高校英语选修课系列教材

ENGLISH FOR BUSINESS COMMUNICATION

商务交际 英语教程

主　编　于红霞
副主编　王欣双　尹雪梅　张　聪
　　　　孙丽霞　白金凤

U0365811

清华大学出版社

北京

内 容 简 介

本教材旨在帮助学生全面提升商务英语综合能力以及商务环境下的英语交际能力。全书共分14个单元，内容基本涵盖了商务交际活动中出现的常见话题，从商务活动着手，依次介绍了新创意、公司、工作方式、商务会议、顾客、订单及付款、广告、商务旅行、产品展示、物流、员工管理、商业道德以及全球化相关商务话题。本书中的音频以二维码的形式呈现，读者可直接用手机扫码听音。

本教材商务知识介绍简洁凝练，语言技能训练类型丰富，是学生短时间内快速掌握商务英语基本知识和技能的有效工具。

图书在版编目（CIP）数据

商务交际英语教程 / 于红霞主编 . —北京：清华大学出版社，2022.4
高校英语选修课系列教材
ISBN 978-7-302-56770-7

Ⅰ.①商… Ⅱ.①于… Ⅲ.①商务-英语-高等学校-教材 Ⅳ.①F7

中国版本图书馆 CIP 数据核字（2020）第 211845 号

责任编辑：钱屹芝
封面设计：子　一
责任校对：王凤芝
责任印制：杨　艳

出版发行：清华大学出版社
　　　　网　　址：http://www.tup.com.cn, http://www.wqbook.com
　　　　地　　址：北京清华大学学研大厦 A 座　　邮　　编：100084
　　　　社 总 机：010-83470000　　　　　　　　邮　　购：010-62786544
　　　　投稿与读者服务：010-62776969, c-service@tup.tsinghua.edu.cn
　　　　质量反馈：010-62772015, zhiliang@tup.tsinghua.edu.cn
印 装 者：三河市金元印装有限公司
经　　销：全国新华书店
开　　本：185mm×260mm　　印　　张：12.5　　字　　数：254千字
版　　次：2022 年 6 月第 1 版　　　　　印　　次：2022 年 6 月第 1 次印刷
定　　价：69.00 元

产品编号：087303-01

本教材由"2019 年度大连外国语大学学科建设专项经费资助项目"支持，在此表示感谢！

前　言

　　进入 21 世纪，经济全球化进一步发展，互联网经济蓬勃兴起。中国与外界的合作日益加深的同时，也面临着诸多机遇与挑战。在这个大背景下，高等教育的人才培养朝着国际化、多元化、个性化和跨学科方向发展。各高校都在努力探索新的人才培养路径，力争为社会培养英语语言基本功扎实、具有较强的商务交际能力和创新精神的新型人才。本教材便是在这个大背景下应运而生。

　　本教材的主要编写目的是为学生提供相关的国际商务背景知识，训练学生听、说、读、写、译的英语综合运用能力，提高学生商务环境下的英语交际能力。全书共分 14 个单元，内容涵盖了商务交际活动中的常见话题，从商务活动着手，依次介绍了新创意、公司、工作方式、商务会议、顾客、订单及付款、广告、商务旅行、产品展示、物流、员工管理、商业道德以及全球化等商务话题。各个单元彼此独立，又相互关联，承前启后，由浅入深。每个单元分为六个板块：词汇、阅读、听力、翻译、写作及延展阅读。各个板块均设计了多种练习，以强化学生的商务英语语言能力。本教材商务知识介绍简洁凝练，语言技能训练类型丰富，是学生短时间内快速掌握商务英语基本知识和技能的有效工具。

　　本教材具有以下特点：

　　1. **专题性**：本教材选取的主题覆盖商务活动的主要方面。精选文章既介绍基础知识又有扩展阅读，揭示商务活动要旨，使学生能在短时间内了解相关商务活动，为今后学习及工作打下基础。

　　2. **实用性**：本教材除向学生介绍基本商务知识外，依据语言学习规律，从听、说、读、写、译五个方面设计学习任务，提高学生的语言交际技能，全面训练学生的综合语言运用能力。任务设计均基于商务活动中可能出现的情景，更具实用性。

　　3. **可读性**：本教材精选英文主流媒体的文章，语言地道、通俗易懂，文章可读性强。文章中专业性强的词汇还配了注释。

　　本教材既可作为各高校英语类专业学生补充商务知识、提升商务英语技能的必修课或选修课教材，也可作为非语言类专业学生提升相关知识和技能的选修课教材。同时，本教材也用于学生准备剑桥商务英语证书（BEC）考试，作为备考、自学用书，助力学生获取求职、晋升的"通行证"。

本教材是 2019 年度大连外国语大学学科建设专项经费资助项目。本教材的编者来自大连外国语大学、东北财经大学以及大连医科大学从事商务英语教学的一线教师，有着丰富的教学经验。同时，外贸行业的业内人士参与了教材的设计与审定，确保教材内容与现实中的商务世界紧密相连。

本教材编写过程中参考了很多现有的商务英语相关教材，并引用了一些网络资源。在此，我们谨向这些书籍和文章的作者由衷地表示感谢。鉴于本书的编者学术水平及编写经验有限，书中难免有疏漏或不妥之处，恳请使用或阅读本书的各位专家、老师和广大读者批评指正。

于红霞

2021 年 12 月于大连

Contents

Unit 1
Introduction to Business Activities

Business activity, also known as business operation, encompasses all the economic activities carried out by a company during the course of business. It includes things like buying, selling, marketing or investing for the purpose of generating profits or developing economic opportunities.

Learning Objectives

* To make a list of activities involved in business;
* To discuss the general activities in the business world;
* To spot details about running business while listening;
* To compose a notice with correct layout and structure.

Warm-up questions

(1) What is business?

(2) What activities are involved in business?

Part A
General business vocabulary

1. Match the words in the box with the following descriptions.

A. distribution	B. supply	C. demand	D. advertising
E. marketing	F. production	G. profit	H. customer

(1) This financial benefit is realized when the amount of revenue gained from a business activity exceeds the expenses, costs and taxes. It will go to the business owner, who may or may not decide to spend it on the business.

(2) Basically it is finding out what buyers want or need and then getting it to them, to the profit or benefit of everyone involved in the transaction.

(3) It refers to the producer's (or seller's) ability and willingness to sell or produce specific quantities of a good in a given time period.

(4) This is the process of converting resources into a form in which people need or want them.

(5) It refers to the movement of goods and services from the source through a distribution channel, right up to the final customer, consumer, or user, and the movement of payment in the opposite direction, right up to the original producer or supplier.

(6) In economics, this term means the utility for goods or services of an economic agent, relative to his/her income.

(7) It is a form of marketing communication used to promote or sell something, usually a business product or service.

(8) It refers to a person, a company, or another entity which buys goods and services produced by another person, company, or another entity.

2. **Listen to the conversations and answer the questions.**

(1) Where does the conversation probably take place?

(2) How long will the guest stay in this place?

(3) What kind of business does the visitor's company do?

(4) Who does Nicole Bryant want to see?

(5) What does Mr. Jones try to do?

(6) What product is the representative from the Coca Cola company interested in?

(7) Will Ms. Oliver look at everything closely in the showroom?

(8) Is Addison satisfied with the samples?

Part B
Reading

What Is Business

[1] We can define business broadly as all the work in providing people with goods and services for a profit. This definition, of course, is very broad indeed, since that work can include an enormous variety of tasks.

The activities involved in business

[2] If you had an idea for the *proverbial* better *mousetrap*, you would have to do a great deal of practical work before your *brainstorm* could become a reality. First of all, you would have to acquire the necessary resources—wood and metal, tools, a *workshop*, *and the like*. Then you would have to organize the actual production—devising an efficient *assembly* process, training your worker, and *supervising* the operation. After this (assuming the world wasn't *beating a path* to your door), you would need to *distribute* your product to as many stores as possible, and then make the public aware of its existence and superior qualities. Finally—or, actually, before you did anything else—you would have to find money to get the whole *enterprise* started. Equipment and materials must be bought, workers paid, *distribution* and advertising paid for—before you could sell a single mousetrap.

[3] This *sequence* of tasks, needless to say, is a simplified outline of the kinds of activities involved in business. In general terms, though, it is typical of businesses of all sizes whatever the nature of the enterprise. An icecream company offers a product. An airline offers a service. But both need to acquire resources, produce what they intend to sell,

advertise it, and make it available to customers.

[4] The estimated 16 million American businesses come in all forms and sizes. From *General Motors Corporation*, which has over 1 million *shareholders*, 700,000 employees, and 41 billion in *assets*, to the one-man hot dog cart on a busy street corner, the business scene is constantly changing. New products and services are forever being offered by *entrepreneurs* looking to make a million. Most don't make it, but people keep trying.

Business as a profit-making activity

[5] We describe business as all the work involved in providing people with goods and services for a profit. The last three words are import. Profit, simply put, is the money left over from all sums received from sales after expenses have been *deducted*. If it costs you $1.00 to produce one of your mousetraps and you sell it for $1.50, your profit is fifty cents (before taxes, of course).

[6] The element of profit is the foundation of our economic system. It is indeed, the whole point—the "bottom line" for most business activities and enterprises. The American economic system is based on the idea that the owner of a business is entitled to keep whatever profits the business produces. It takes effort, after all, to put a desirable product or service into a useful form and then sell it to people. Furthermore, the owner may have to take a *considerable* financial risk. Most businesses need a *substantial* investment to get started, and if a new *venture* doesn't succeed (and most don't), whoever *financed* it stands to lose a great deal of money. It seems only fair, therefore, that someone who makes the effort and takes the financial risk should be rewarded with the profits.

[7] At this point we must note that not all businesses exist to make a profit. As we'll see, it is the nature of the American system to provide goods and services for which there is a sizable demand or for which a relatively small number of people are willing to spend a large sum of money. But some small *segments* of society have needs that *profit-oriented* businesses can't afford to supply at prices that these markets can pay. Therefore, our society supports a number of nonprofit businesses, such as *the Rand Corporations* and *Goodwill Industries*. In other *respects*, these enterprises are much like profit-directed businesses.

Adapted from *Business Today (Fourth Edition)*

New words and expressions

assembly	[ə'semblɪ]	*n.*	装配；集会，集合
asset	['æset]	*n.*	资产
brainstorm	['breɪnstɔːm]	*n.*	集思广益；头脑风暴
considerable	[kən'sɪdərəbəl]	*adj.*	相当大的；重要的，值得考虑的
deduct	[dɪ'dʌkt]	*vt.*	扣除，减去
distribute	[dɪ'strɪbjuːt]	*vt.*	分配；散布
distribution	[dɪstrɪ'bjuːʃn]	*n.*	分布；分配；分销
enterprise	['entəpraɪz]	*n.*	企业；事业
entrepreneur	[ˌɒntrəprə'nɜː(r)]	*n.*	企业家；创业者
finance	[faɪ'næns]	*vt.*	负担经费，供给……经费
mousetrap	['maʊstræp]	*n.*	捕鼠器
profit-oriented	['prɒfɪt'ɔːrɪentɪd]	*adj.*	利润导向，效益导向，营利性的
proverbial	[prə'vɜːbɪəl]	*adj.*	众所周知的，有名的
respect	[rɪ'spekt]	*n.*	方面
segment	['segmənt]	*n.*	段；部分
sequence	['siːkwəns]	*n.*	序列；顺序
shareholder	['ʃeəhəʊldə]	*n.*	股东；股票持有人
substantial	[səb'stænʃ(ə)l]	*adj.*	大量的；实质的；内容充实的
supervise	['suːpəvaɪz]	*vt.*	监督，管理；指导
venture	['ventʃə]	*n.*	企业；风险；冒险
workshop	['wɜːkʃɒp]	*n.*	车间；工场
and the like			等等；以此类推
beat a path			开辟一条路

General Motors Corporation　通用汽车公司。通用汽车公司成立于 1908 年 9 月 16 日，自从威廉·杜兰特创建了美国通用汽车公司以来，通用汽车在全球生产和销售包括雪佛兰、别克、凯迪拉克、宝骏、霍顿、欧宝、沃克斯豪尔以及五菱等一系列品牌车型并提供服务。通用汽车旗下多个品牌全系列车型畅销于全球 120 多个国家和地区，包括电动车、微车、重型卡车、紧凑型车及敞篷车。

Goodwill Industries　善念机构。该机构目前是全球最大的非营利经营型慈善组织之一。

the Rand Corporations　兰德公司。该公司是美国最重要的以军事为主的综合性战略研究机构。兰德公司正式成立于 1948 年 11 月，总部设在美国加利福尼亚州的圣莫尼卡，在华盛顿设有办事处，负责与政府联系。

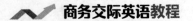

Reading comprehension

1. Work in pairs and discuss the following questions according to the passage.

    (1) What do you normally have to consider before your brainstorm becomes a reality?

    (2) Why is the business scene constantly changing?

    (3) What does business mean according to this passage?

    (4) What will the entrepreneur get if the business succeeds? What will he or she lose if it fails?

    (5) Why are there some non-profit businesses?

2. Choose the best answers to explain the meanings of the underlined words.

    (1) You would have to acquire the necessary resources—wood and metal, tools, a <u>workshop</u>, and the like.

        A. machinery   B. workplace   C. training course   D. device

    (2) Then you would have to organize the actual production—devising an efficient assembly process, training your worker, and <u>supervising</u> the operation.

        A. directing   B. operating   C. trying   D. imitating

    (3) Finally—or, actually, before you did anything else—you would have to find money to get the whole <u>enterprise</u> started.

        A. unit   B. venture   C. branch   D. subsidiary

    (4) This <u>sequence</u> of tasks, needless to say, is a simplified outline of the kinds of activities involved in business.

        A. order   B. line   C. series   D. bunch

    (5) New products and services are forever being offered by <u>entrepreneurs</u> looking to make a million.

        A. interpreters   B. entries   C. entertainers   D. business people

    (6) Profit, simply put, is the money left over from all sums received from sales after expenses have been <u>deducted</u>.

        A. subtracted   B. deduced   C. demonstrated   D. subsidized

    (7) Furthermore, the owner may have to take a <u>considerable</u> financial risk.

        A. consider   B. huge   C. considerate   D. considering

    (8) If a new venture doesn't succeed (and most don't), whoever <u>financed</u> stands to lose a great deal of money.

        A. found   B. supervised   C. supported... financially   D. faced

    (9) But some small <u>segments</u> of society have needs that profit-oriented businesses can't afford to supply at prices that these markets can pay.

        A. segmentations   B. sanctions   C. seductions   D. groups

10) In other <u>respects</u>, these enterprises are much like profit-directed businesses.

    A. aspects   **B.** respected   **C.** points   **D.** respective

Part C
Listening

Listen to the business story "Turning a Hobby into Business". Decide whether the following statements are True (T) or False (F).

(1) Rusty won the "Seattle Best Dessert" award for twice in these years.

(2) Rusty's cheesecake business is his first trial in business.

(3) In order to keep his overheads low, Rusty uses his own kitchen.

(4) Rusty sells his cheesecake wholesale in retail markets, and in restaurants.

(5) To get feedback from customers, Rusty talks to the customers directly.

New words and expressions

accolade	['ækəleɪd]	*n.*	荣誉；称赞
align	[ə'laɪn]	*vt.*	使成一行；匹配
		vi.	排列；排成一行
batch	[bætʃ]	*n.*	一批；一炉；一次所制之量
bootstrap	['buːtstræp]	*n.*	【计】引导程序，辅助程序
deli	['delɪ]	*n.*	熟食店（等于 delicatessen）
dessert	[dɪ'zɜːt]	*n.*	餐后甜点，甜点心
entrepreneurial	[ˌɒntrəprə'nɜːrɪəl]	*adj.*	企业家的，创业者的
feedback	['fiːdbæk]	*n.*	反馈，回复；成果；资料
full-blown	[fʊl'bləʊn]	*adj.*	成熟的；（花）盛开的；（帆等）张满的
idle	['aɪdl]	*adj.*	闲置的；懒惰的；停顿的
ingredient	[ɪn'griːdɪənt]	*n.*	原料；要素；组成部分
overhead	[ˌəʊvə'hed]	*n.*	【会计】经常费用；间接费用
passionate	['pæʃənət]	*adj.*	热情的；激昂的；易怒的

perfect	[pə'fekt]	vt.	使完美；使熟练
quest	[kwest]	n.	探索；追求
recipe	['resɪpɪ]	n.	食谱；秘诀；烹饪法
scale	[skeɪl]	vt.	确定规模；依比例决定
ultra-premium	['ʌltrə'priːmɪəm]	adj.	顶级的
in a row			连续，一连串
trial and error			反复试验；尝试错误法

Part D
Translating

Translate the following sentences into English.

(1) 大多数企业以营利为目的。

(2) 国际贸易是指在多个国家进行的业务，包括购买、销售商品和服务。

(3) 最赚钱的公司并不是把利润放在第一位的公司。

(4) 人们对投资回报的预期大大降低。

(5) 创业风险很高，但回报也很高。

Part E
Writing skills: Notice

写作提示

公告（Notice）是一种正式文体，用来告知、展示、提醒或警告相关重要事项。在商业领域中，公告既可用在企业内部上级对下级、组织对成员或平行单位之间部署工作、传达事项、召开会议等，也可以用于企业对公众介绍其产品、服务以及公司活动等事项。

公告的写法有两种，一种是以布告形式在宣传板、网站上贴出，把事情通知给有关人员等；另一种是以书信的形式，发给有关人员，写作形式同普通书信，写明通知的具体内容。

公告一般包含以下信息：事件、地点、发生时间、参加人员、联系人（发布机构）。信息应简洁、清晰，不引起歧义、误解，信息表达充分。

公告格式：

1）发布公告的组织或公司：一般位于正文开头居中。

2）公告标志：标志一般要醒目，多用 NOTICE 作标题。

3）发布日期一般写在标题 NOTICE 的下一行，或文末。

4）公告正文：写明事项的具体时间、地点、概括性内容、出席对象及有关注意事项。正文表述可采用叙述形式。也可以用广告形式突出某个部分（如主题、任务、时间、地点）。文字力求简明扼要，一个句子成分可分为几行书写，分行书写时，尽量居中，各行的第一个字母必须大写。

5）联系人员信息：包含必要的联系方式，如电话、电子邮箱及网站等。

Example

BURNABY CIVIC EMPLOYEES' UNION
C.U.P.E. LOCAL 23
NOTICE

February 12, 2020

Precarious Workers Committee Meeting

Date: Tuesday, March 29, 2020

Time: 5:30 pm

Place: Burnaby Civic Employees' Union

#110-4938 Canada Way, Burnaby

AGENDA

— Proposed brochure and website

— General Business

— Information booths (hats off parade, etc.)

— CUPE Local 23 Elections

—AGM Report

For more information, contact the Union office

E-mail: admin@ burnabyunion.ca

Tel: 604-397-0200

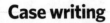
Case writing

Task: Metta Toy Co. Ltd. is organising a year-end-sales meeting. The notice should include the following issues:

* Time: 9.30-11.30am, December 18
* Place: Rm 208
* Drink and snacks provided

You are asked to write the notice. Think about other matters that should also be stated in it. Write in about **40-50** words.

Part F
Further business story

Start Your Own Small Business

Wouldn't it be great to be able to quit your job, be your own boss and earn a paycheck from the comfort of your own home? The good news is that with a little planning and some startup money, it is possible! Let's delve a little deeper into how to start a small business from home and help you decide how much planning and money you'll need to be your own boss.

Creating the concept

Before quitting their jobs, the potential entrepreneurs must first think of a concept, product or service to ***generate*** a steady income. And while that may sound easy, it's not. You should ***conceive*** a plan that puts your knowledge, experience and expertise to use but in a way that allows you to make the most amount of your money.

When first thinking of some business ideas, start with areas you already have a great deal of interest, equipment and materials for. This will help cut down on the ***startup costs*** for your company and also let you ***hit the ground running*** when you do ***hang out your shingle***. Also, ***peruse*** the local paper and advertisements to see what other types of businesses are out there. Are there other similar businesses in your neighborhood or is there a business area that is lacking?

Doing something you like isn't the only consideration. You need to get an idea of the prospects for the potential business. Is it a business with a market? Can you make money at it? This will require some research into the marketplace as well as how other similar businesses have ***fared***.

Developing a work space

Your home is where you live. This means that its primary function is to serve as a *dwelling* for you and your family—not as a warehouse or meeting place for your business and its clients. Make certain that if you are considering entering the manufacturing business (for example) that your *garage* or *shed* is large enough to handle your work—without forcing your family and your vehicles into stormy weather.

Similarly, if your work will be computer-based, make sure that you have the technology necessary to give your idea a fighting chance. In addition, make sure that you have a *dedicated* area that's cut off from the rest of the house and that can afford you some privacy. Remember, hearing a barking dog or a crying baby in the background when you are trying to work or meet with a client may not be ideal for you or your family.

Outsourcing partners/employees

While it would be great to be the *sole owner* of your company and have complete control of every aspect, sometimes a lack of funds or experience makes it necessary to have a partner. In this case, consider someone that is bright will represent the company well, and has some sort of expertise in the business you are developing, be it sales, marketing, *book-keeping*, or other financial matters.

Also, try to define the tasks that you and your partner(s) will be responsible for before opening up shop. That way, there will be fewer disagreements and the business will operate more smoothly. Also, make sure that all partners are legally cared for by the company, and that the proper forms are filed with the *regulatory authorities*—this may mean filing twice and paying for title changes if you need to find a new partner, but it will protect both of you in the long run.

Next, decide if you'll need employees—whether now or in the future. If so, put some thought into how you will get them and what you will pay them for their work. Also, think about how you'll *do payroll*, and whether people will want to work from your home, from their own homes or if you'll need to find another facility to house them.

Doing your research

Some books on forming a small business suggest that after *hatching* an idea, an entrepreneur should just "go for it". However, this bold approach could land you in some shaky territory.

Instead, a good first move is to start asking family and friends what they think about your small business idea. Consider asking them specific questions such as:
• Would you purchase this particular product and/or service?

- What do you think its worth?

- What is the best way to market the idea?

- Is this something that you think is a *fad*, or do you feel it could be a *viable* business for the long term?

- Is there anything you can think of to improve this idea?

- What other businesses in this field have you heard of or do you currently use for this product/service?

If you're married and/or have kids, you should also be asking your family how they feel about you quitting your job and working from home. This will affect them on a psychological and financial level. If any of their answers are negative, you should spend some time discussing their concerns and decide whether your goal is worth continuing against their wishes.

After obtaining all of this feedback, go back to the drawing board and see if the idea can be improved upon so that your product or service can be differentiated from the competition. Remember, you want to hit the ground running and *turn* as many *heads* as possible when first starting off!

Finding funding

Once you have an idea and the approval of your family, you need to decide how you are going to finance it. Most businesses will need at least a little startup income. This investment will hopefully help you *break even* after a year, but keep in mind that even successful businesses can remain in *deficit* for the first few years. Because of this, you will want to *tap into* a few different sources of funding. Some of these include:

- A small-business loan

- Savings

- Money generated from other investments

- Family/friends who will act as investors

- Personal loan from the bank

- *Home equity loan*

- Credit cards (as a last resort)

Source capital that won't *hamper* your longer-term security. In other words, try to avoid *racking up* costly credit card debt that could cost 20% or more in yearly interest fees.

Finally, one of the best things you can do before you take the entrepreneurial leap is to build up an emergency fund to fall back on if your company doesn't break even for a few months. Three months of living expenses is a minimum goal for a new business owner, but even more will help take the stress off of you and let you spend your energy on your company.

Covering your bases

All business owners should think about what would happen to the enterprise and the *revenue streams* being generated if health or other issues were to prevent them from being involved in the business. In other words, if the entrepreneur were to become disabled, who would take over? Could the business survive?

Consider these issues beforehand and determine whether disability income insurance makes sense, or if a partner could fill the *void* caused by your absence.

Foreseeing the future

It's great to own a business, but ultimately the entrepreneur will probably want to retire or move on to other challenges. With that in mind, you should create a business plan that discusses how you will *transfer*, sell or close your company. If your business depends on your unique knowledge and contacts, it may not be able to be *assumed* by another party.

Conclusion

There are few things more satisfying and rewarding than launching and owning your own home-based business, but before diving in, be sure to do your homework. Making a business work is not an easy task, but proper planning will help to increase its chances of success.

New words and expressions

assume	*vt.*	夺取；擅用
book-keeping	*n.*	簿记，记账
conceive	*vt.*	构想，设想
dedicated	*adj.*	专用的
deficit	*n.*	赤字
delve	*vi.*	钻研；探究
dwelling	*n.*	住处；寓所
fad	*n.*	时尚；一时的爱好；一时流行的狂热
fare	*vi.*	经营；进展
garage	*n.*	车库
generate	*vt.*	产生，形成
hamper	*vt.*	妨碍；束缚

hatch	vt.	孵；策划
peruse	vt.	仔细阅读
shed	n.	小屋，棚
transfer	vt.	转让；转移；传递
viable	adj.	可行的
void	n.	空虚；空间；空隙
break even		不赚不赔，收支相抵，收支平衡
do payroll		计算工资
hang out one's shingle		挂牌营业
hit the ground running		（非正式）积极着手进行
home equity loan		住房净值贷款
rack up		击倒，获胜
regulatory authority		法规机构
revenue stream		收入来源；收益流
sole owner		唯一拥有人，独资所有人
startup cost		开办费用；启动成本
tap into		获得
turn heads		引人注目

Critical thinking

Work in groups and discuss the following questions.

(1) Do you want to start your own business? Why or Why not?

(2) What kind of business would you do if you are going to start your own business?

(3) What preparations should you make when you start a business?

Unit 2
New Ideas

New ideas aren't necessarily the result of highly-paid think tanks or drug-induced vision quests in the desert. Often they are unexpected moments of inspiration that help keep companies in business. The big challenge of generating new ideas is freeing yourself from the conventional thoughts. Brainstorming is one of effective approaches for people to stimulate their new idea generators and come up with creative solutions to problems.

Learning objectives

* To learn vocabulary of generating new ideas;
* To discuss brainstorming topics with idiomatic words and expressions;
* To be equipped with listening expressions about innovation;
* To comprehend the format and tips of composing notes.

Warm-up questions

(1) Why are new ideas so important in business world?

(2) What are effective approaches to fostering new ideas?

Part A
General business vocabulary

1. Match the words in the box with the following descriptions.

> A. vein   B. collaboration   C. stakeholder   D. brainstorming
>
> E. campaign   F. commodity   G. ideation   H. sector

(1) It is the capacity for or the act of forming or entertaining ideas.

(2) The purpose of the act is to work with another person or group of people to create or produce something.

(3) It refers to a particular style or manner.

(4) It is a series of planned activities with a particular social, commercial or political aim.

(5) Someone has invested money into something, or has some important connection with it, and therefore is affected by its success or failure.

(6) It is a part or a branch of a particular area of activity, especially of a country's economy.

(7) The activity is that a group of people meet in order to try to develop ideas and think of ways of solving problems.

(8) It is an article, product or material that is exchanged in international trade.

2. Listen to the conversations and answer the questions.

(1) What is the result of the second speaker's work in ABC Corporation?

(2) What are they talking about?

(3) What is the second speaker's idea of the relationship between brainstorming and planning?

(4) What is the drawback to brainstorming according to the second speaker?

(5) What will the first speaker do?

(6) What is the super tool?

(7) Why does the second speaker say that the field of innovation is slow to make progress?

(8) Why does the first speaker want to distinguish between the noun "innovation" and the verb "innovating"?

Part B
Reading

Why Brainstorming Is a Crucial Element in Business

[1] Brainstorming is defined as "the *mulling over* of ideas by one or more individuals in an attempt to devise or find a solution to a problem". With just this definition, it's easy to see that brainstorming, and brainstorming successfully, is vital to the success of a business.

[2] *Ideation*, or commonly known as idea generation, is something of a *commodity* in business. After so many years, with many different varieties of new technologies, how does a new business come into the industry and make an impact? Or *in the* same *vein*, how does an established business continue to grow and develop to suit their customer base? Brainstorming is a key component of successful idea generation in business.

[3] There are a *multitude* of uses for brainstorming. Most people associate brainstorming with new product ideas or marketing campaigns—but brainstorming can also be used for tasks including internal procedures, company structures and written articles. It all depends on the type of business and the approach that business takes to *collaborations*. There are, of course, many other ways that these types of issues could be resolved—so why bother with brainstorming? Here are three key reasons.

Collecting viewpoints

[4] The best way to find out how people feel about a product line, a service offering, the way in which a company is structured or even internal processes is fairly obvious—ask them! As a manager, your viewpoint may be different to that of the people actioning a particular service or process. If you're not involved in management, then be aware that managers aren't able to understand everything involved in the day-to-day requirements. Brainstorming and collecting the viewpoints of others help to create ideas and *innovations*

that are widely respected within a business.

Encouraging thoughts

[5] Similar to the above, inviting the wider *stakeholders* of a company into brainstorming encourages employees at all levels to think critically about current issues or future goals—and this is likely to feed into their future *endeavors* within a company.

Building team relationships

[6] Instead of one person feeling the pressure to come up with an amazing new idea, brainstorming allows employees to share the load of innovation, and encourages employees to work together respectfully and responsibly, to develop ideas and create *viable* solutions to problems. If these employees are from different *sectors* within a business, this also encourages inter-office staff to share their views on a particular issue—increasing understanding across the business.

[7] These are three main ways that brainstorming can benefit the continuing *evolution* of your business. But how do you then build an environment that encourages brainstorming?

[8] There are no set rules or regulations for brainstorming *sessions*—that's part of the beauty of it. But there are a few things you can do to create a culture of brainstorming and idea generation in your workplace.

- Avoid judging ideas immediately

[9] People are far more likely to share their ideas and visions in a comfortable and supportive space—arrange to include all ideas, record all ideas, and make the time to judge them on their merits at a later date. People need to feel able to share any ideas they may have—create an *inclusive* and *non-judgmental* space to *accommodate*.

- Encourage a little "crazy"

[10] In a similar vein to the point above, remember to encourage a few wild ideas from your staff and stakeholders. These so-called "crazy" ideas can be adjusted later, if required—but remember that many of the world's best inventions and creations came from a *bizarre* idea. Be open to exploring everything.

- Think of ideas as building blocks

[11] Nobody comes into a brainstorming session with the world's most perfect, affordable, useful and marketable product or service in mind. Allow your *brainstormers* to build on each other's ideas—often, another person's idea is what sparks someone else's creativity. Many ideas can be combined and integrated to great effect and allow the idea to develop organically wherever possible.

- Keep focused on the task at hand

[12] If you're part of a growing business, with many exciting opportunities, then that is fantastic —but it can be very *detrimental* to successful brainstorming. If you're holding a brainstorming meeting for a particular issue, perhaps around themes for a coming event, then ensure that your discussions stay focused on that, and don't *veer* into *unchartered* territory like product ideas for the coming year. Keep confusion to a minimum.

- Create a display

[13] Visuals are a great addition to brainstorming meetings—arrange for a whiteboard or colorful stationery supplies for those involved. This will help people to connect images to their ideas, and build on the ideas of others.

[14] These are just a few ideas to help implement a well-organized brainstorming session—but it's definitely not an *exhaustive* list.

New words and expressions

accommodate	[ə'kɒmədeɪt]	*vt.*	容纳；（使）适应
bizarre	[bɪ'zɑ:]	*adj.*	奇异的
collaboration	[kə,læbə'reɪʃn]	*n.*	合作
commodity	[kə'mɒdəti]	*n.*	商品，货物
detrimental	[,detrɪ'mentl]	*adj.*	不利的；有害的
endeavor	[ɪn'devə]	*n.*	努力；尽力
evolution	[,i:və'lu:ʃn]	*n.*	演变；进展
exhaustive	[ɪg'zɔ:stɪv]	*adj.*	详尽的
ideation	[,aɪdɪ'eɪʃn]	*n.*	构思过程
inclusive	[ɪn'klu:sɪv]	*adj.*	包括的，包含的
innovation	[,ɪnə'veɪʃn]	*n.*	创新；新方法
multitude	['mʌltɪtju:d]	*n.*	多数
non-judgmental	['nɒn,dʒʌdʒ'mentl]	*adj.*	非主观的；无偏见的
sector	['sektə]	*n.*	部门
session	['seʃn]	*n.*	会议
stakeholder	['steɪkhəʊldə(r)]	*n.*	利益相关者
unchartered	[ʌn'tʃɑ:təd]	*adj.*	未得特许状的；不合规则的
veer	[vɪə]	*vi.*	（使）转向；改变观点
viable	['vaɪəbl]	*adj.*	可行的
in the... vein			以……的方式
mull over			仔细考虑

Reading comprehension

1. Work in pairs and discuss the following questions according to the passage.

(1) What is brainstorming?

(2) Why is brainstorming an integral part in business world?

(3) How can a manager find out people's ideas of a product line or a service offering?

(4) What is suggested by the author for creating a culture of brainstorming?

(5) What is the function of visuals in the brainstorming meetings?

2. Choose the best answers to explain the meanings of the underlined words.

(1) He warned it would have a <u>detrimental</u> effect on the numbers of doctors entering the profession.

    A. determined   B. deteriorated   C. destructive   D. harmful

(2) We've told them this thing was not financially <u>viable</u> and they won't listen to the government.

    A. practical   B. valuable   C. sensible   D. meaningless

(3) There are a <u>multitude</u> of online and offline classes and groups that teach programming.

    A. vocation   B. measurement   C. large number   D. coordination

(4) The academy takes the <u>endeavor</u> seriously enough to protect that remarkably rigorous voting process.

    A. enrichment   B. struggle   C. reasoning   D. predictor

(5) Thomas insists that it is more about cultural grounding than a conscious decision not to <u>integrate</u>.

    A. combine   B. reinforce   C. prolong   D. compel

(6) The psychologists show that people take mental shortcuts that cause them to <u>veer</u> from rational behavior.

    A. abolish   B. accompany   C. swerve   D. chase

(7) The festival seeks to <u>resolve</u> conflict, strengthen community bonds and hopefully, arrive at a greater peace.

    A. cover   B. regard   C. launch   D. settle

(8) Doors in the building were designed to be extra tall to <u>accommodate</u> the famously towering players.

    A. hold   B. annoy   C. fracture   D. disrupt

(9) Microsoft is committed to openness, <u>innovation</u> and the protection of privacy on the Internet.

    A. mainstream   B. prominence

    C. creativeness   D. acknowledgement

(10) They explain the <u>bizarre</u> name of the company, just in case the customer is confused.

    A. responsible   **B.** fantastic   **C.** fragile   **D.** formal

Part C
Listening

Listen to innovation lessons from Pixar "An Interview with Oscar-winning Director Brad Bird". Decide whether the following statements are True (T) or False (F).

(1) Brad Bird was hired by the Pixar because his movie *The Iron Giant* had been a big hit.

(2) The creative heads in Pixar were excited about the idea of the film *The Incredibles*, but once Brad Bird showed story reels of exactly what he wanted, the technical teams felt these effects were difficult to achieve.

(3) All different departments of the company are involved in making a film and the role of the director is to find a way to get them to put forth creativity in a harmonious way.

(4) From Bird's perspective, one should do definite things that are not at the edge of one's capabilities.

(5) Pixar arranges everything carefully in order to stimulate a creative culture.

New words and expressions

animator	['ænɪmeɪtə]	*n.*	卡通片绘制者
atrium	['eɪtrɪəm]	*n.*	中庭，天井前厅
complacency	[kəm'pleɪs(ə)nsɪ]	*n.*	自满；满足
complacent	[kəm'pleɪs(ə)nt]	*adj.*	自满的；得意的
foster	['fɒstə]	*vt.*	培养
hands-on	[ˌhændz'ɒn]	*adj.*	亲身实践的，亲自动手的
insidiously	[ɪn'sɪdɪəslɪ]	*adv.*	阴险地
malcontent	['mælkəntent]	*n.*	不满现状的人；反抗者
morale	[mə'rɑːl]	*n.*	士气，斗志
nurture	['nɜːtʃə]	*vt.*	鼓励
orchestra	['ɔːkɪstrə]	*n.*	管弦乐队
passionate	['pæʃnət]	*adj.*	热情的；热烈的

probe	[prəʊb]	*vi.*	探查
unhinged	[ʌn'hindʒd]	*adj.*	精神错乱的
black sheep			败家子；害群之马

Edwin Catmull	艾德文·卡特姆，美国计算机科学家，迪士尼动画工作室和皮克斯动画工作室现任总裁，皮克斯的创始人之一。作为计算机科学家，卡特姆为计算机图形学做出了许多重大的贡献。
John Lasseter	约翰·拉塞特，美国的动画师、电影导演、皮克斯动画工作室和迪士尼动画工作室的首席创意官以及迪士尼幻想工程的首席创意顾问。很多人把他看作"当代的华特·迪士尼"。
Pixar	皮克斯动画工作室，简称皮克斯，是一家位于加州爱莫利维尔市的计算机动画制片厂。皮克斯的前身是卢卡斯影业于 1979 年成立的电脑动画部。1986 年，苹果公司联合创始人史蒂夫·乔布斯收购了卢卡斯的电脑动画部，成立了皮克斯动画工作室。2006 年，皮克斯被迪士尼以 74 亿美元收购，成为华特·迪士尼公司的一部分，乔布斯亦因此成为迪士尼的最大个人股东。
Steve Jobs	史蒂夫·乔布斯，美国企业家、营销家和发明家，苹果公司的联合创始人之一，曾任董事长及首席执行官职位，NeXT 创办人及首席执行官，也是皮克斯动画的创办人并曾任首席执行官，2006 年为华特·迪士尼公司的董事会成员。
The Incredibles	《超人总动员》，由皮克斯动画工作室制作，是迪士尼公司发行的第六部长篇电脑动画。本片由布拉德·伯德（Brad Bird）导演，迈克·吉亚奇诺（Michael Giacchino）配乐，于 2004 年上映，获第 77 届奥斯卡最佳动画片奖。

Part D
Translating

Translate the following sentences into English.

(1) 头脑风暴是一个重要工具，若有效地实施，可以在任何层面得到具有想象力的结果。

(2) 头脑风暴的核心在于小组成员提出自己的想法且不受批评。

(3) 大多数人把头脑风暴与新产品创意或营销活动联系起来。

(4) 人们可以在大多数情况下使用头脑风暴。

(5) 一些小组成员通常不愿提出自己的想法以避免使自己看起来很愚钝。

(6) 在舒适和友好的气氛下，人们更容易分享他们的想法和见解。

Part E
Writing skills: Note

写作提示

便条（Note）是一种简单的书信，内容简短，大多是临时性的，常见的便条形式有欠条、请假条等。便条的主要目的是尽快地把最新的信息、通知、要求或者活动时间、地点转告给对方。它的特点是用途广、形式简单、文字要求不严格。

商务便条需要注意以下几点：因其时效性，可只写明星期几或者具体时刻，年份可以不写，日期一般写在右上角。由于商务便条不用邮寄，所以不需要写地址。商务便条的内容一般涉及当天或近日的事情，而且没有经过严格事先计划，所以和正规的信函相比，语言比较口语化，结束时可不写结尾礼词，只需写上写便条者的名字即可，不需要写姓。

商务便条写作的基本要求：

1）使用非正式、口语化语言。

2）内容简短，只包含一个主题；切忌内容空洞、言不达意。

3）写作前要对已知信息进行分析归纳，对信息进行加工并恰当使用商务词汇和句式；语法结构要灵活多变，简洁明了。

商务便条没有严格的格式要求和固定格式，可参照下面的格式：

Note	
	Date/Time:
To:	
Message:	

Example

May 20

Mr. Simon,

A customer complained that he had received 150 red color skateboards instead of 100 green and 50 red color skateboards, which had been shipped on May 11. Could you please send me the immediate invoice under contract NO. TXI 2-1 in duplicate?

Aftersales Department

Legeia

Case writing

Task: Mr. Lee is going to buy a large amount of electronic components from your company. He also shows an interest in your company's PCX phone machine, which is in the charge of Mr. Angus Beard, your colleague. Mr. Lee would like to bring 10 samples and some brochures back home to make a trial sale.

Write a short note to Mr. Angus Beard, you should:

* tell him the fact that Mr. Lee is interested in PCX phone;
* mention the number he wants to have;
* suggest their direct contact.

Write in about **40-50** words.

Part F
Further business story

When Dogs Spark Big Ideas

During the past 25 years I have *facilitated* more than 1,000 brainstorming sessions for a wide variety of heavy hitting organizations—everyone from MTV to GE to government think thanks. I've worked with left-brained people, right-brained people, and *reptilian*-brained people.

As you might imagine, I've developed quite a few techniques to get people out of their heads and into a more robust *realm* of possibility. But the biggest breakthroughs I've seen have had less to do with my methods than they did with spontaneous occurrences.

Like the time a *porcelain* hotel dog became the *catalyst* for a game changing product idea.

Here's the deal:

I was leading a daylong ideation session for a large telecommunications company when it was time for lunch. Everyone left the room, visions of tuna wraps in their head, when I noticed a peculiar looking porcelain dog, next to a plastic fern, in the corner of the room—the kind of *kitschy* piece of Americana you'd walk by at a yard sale, *mumbling* under your breath that this was absolutely the last time you'd ever attend a yard sale.

Somehow, I found myself drawn to the dog and, being in a particularly playful mood, picked it up and placed it on a folding chair in the middle of the room.

Tickled by its absolute uselessness and lack of beauty, I put my hat on its weird, little head, and went about my business of getting ready for the afternoon session.

Five minutes later, the head of HR walks into the room, takes off his power tie, and places it, with a *chuckle*, around the dog's neck.

Then an IT guy enters, removes his "Hello My Name Is" *badge* and sticks it on the dog's chest. A well-dressed marketing woman removes her necklace and wraps it around the dog's waist.

There, in the middle of the room, *unleashed*, unbarking, but no longer unloved, sits the perfect brainstorm session *mascot*—a 3D-*embodiment* of our collective mind at that moment in time.

The rest of the participants return soon enough and gather around the porcelain dog as if it was the Holy Grail. A Blackberry gets taped to his back; a scarf gets wrapped around his neck. Someone puts a bandaid over his mouth.

Something is happening that has absolutely nothing to do with my agenda for the day. A curious kind of creativity portal is opening up right before my eyes.

"OK!" I *blurt*, as soon as the last person returns from lunch. "What cool, new product ideas come to mind when you look at a good dog here?"

Ideas start flooding the room. Big ideas. Bold ideas. Totally ridiculous ideas.

In just a few minutes, it is clear that a big idea is emerging—an idea for a *niche* telecommunications market no one in this room has ever considered before—animals—more specifically, dogs who live with blind or disabled people—the kind of dogs who could easily be trained to push a large red button on a one-button phone any time their master was unable to—what soon became known to all of us in that room, as the Paw Phone.

Pet idea conceived, we spend the next ten minutes fleshing it out, adding it to the list of the other big ideas to be presented at the end of the day to an independent focus group.

Isn't it the funny thing? Of the ten ideas we pitched to the focus group that day, the Paw Phone was the third highest rated.

From this experience, we can see that good ideas can come from anyone at any time and any place. While it is impossible to predict precisely when and where the good ideas will manifest, it is possible to predict the conditions that will make it more likely for the good ideas to make their appearance.

In the Paw Phone session, one of these conditions was the spirit of playfulness and *spontaneity* that manifested itself so gloriously during the lunch break.

At that time, I simply followed my hunch that the porcelain dog was, somehow, part of the creative process. I didn't know how things would unfold. I could only trust my instincts and past experience that, often, seemingly random catalysts are the DNA for breakthrough. That, and the fact, that when we manage to enter the state of not trying we often get the best results.

Carl Jung understood this phenomenon: "The creation of something new," he said, "is not accomplished by the intellect, but by the play instinct arising from inner necessity. The creative mind plays with the object it loves."

Play! The creative mind plays with the object it loves! Yes!

And yet, in the corporate world, playfulness is often *demonized*, *marginalized*, and ignored—branded "unprofessional"—as if it was a symptom of the worst kind of anti-business *slacker* mentality.

Indeed, if you find yourself laughing on the job, many of the people around you will think you aren't taking your job seriously. No wonder 62% of all Americans characterize themselves as being dissatisfied with work.

The roots of this weirdness can be traced all the way back to the Garden of Eden.

What happened to Adam when he took a bite of the forbidden fruit? He was condemned, for life, to earning his living by "the sweat of his brow". The free lunch was over. Adam's spontaneity doomed him to a life of heavy lifting and we are the ones who have gotten the *hernia*.

It's time to *shed* the notion that work always has to be so serious—that *grunting* and *groaning* is the preferred response and that laughter, in the workplace, means you're not working.

This just in: Life is supposed to be fun. And since work is a part of life, it too needs to be fun—especially when you find yourself in the middle of a brainstorming session, trying to originate the kind of ideas that will make a difference in the world.

New words and expressions

badge	*n.*	徽章
blurt	*vt.*	未加思索地脱口而出
catalyst	*n.*	催化剂；刺激因素
chuckle	*n.*	轻笑
demonize	*vt.*	妖魔化
embodiment	*n.*	体现；化身
facilitate	*vt.*	促进；帮助；使容易
groan	*vt.*	抱怨
grunt	*vi.*	咕哝着说
hernia	*n.*	疝气
kitschy	*adj.*	艺术上肤浅的
marginalize	*vt.*	排斥
mascot	*n.*	吉祥物
mumble	*vt.*	含糊地说

niche	*n.*	有利可图的市场（或形势等）
porcelain	*n.*	瓷器　*adj.* 瓷制的
realm	*n.*	领域，范围
reptilian	*adj.*	爬虫类的
shed	*vt.*	摆脱
slacker	*n.*	懒鬼
spontaneity	*n.*	自发性
unleash	*vt.*	解除……的束缚

Critical thinking

Work in groups and discuss the following questions.

(1) As a leader of a group, what will you do to encourage your group members to generate new ideas?

(2) What's the relationship between brainstorming and new ideas?

(3) How can you hold a successful brainstorming session?

Unit 3
Company

    A Company is a legal entity made up of an association of person, carrying on a commercial or industrial enterprise. Company members share a common purpose and unite in order to focus their various talents and organize their collectively available skills or resources to achieve specific, declared goals.

    A company or an association of person can be created at law as legal person so that the company in itself can accept limited liability for civil responsibility and taxation incurred as members perform (or fail) to discharge their duty within the publicly declared "birth certificate" or published policy.

Learning objectives

* To incorporate appropriate vocabulary to express ideas about a company;
* To describe the types of business ownership;
* To identify the main ideas and details from a listening text;
* To familiarize with the etiquette and formats of e-mail writing.

(1) What are the types of business ownership?

(2) How much do you know the significance of corporate culture?

Part A
General business vocabulary

1. Match the words or phrases in the box with the following descriptions.

A. board of directors	B. organizational hierarchy
C. internal environment	D. company building
E. managers	F. purchasing
G. Research and Development Department	H. market
I. advertising	J. finance

(1) It refers to an organizational structure in the form of a hierarchy. In an organization, the hierarchy usually consists of a singular/group of power at the top with subsequent levels of power beneath them. Members of hierarchical organizational structures chiefly communicate with their immediate superior and with their immediate subordinates.

(2) It refers to a business office, a place where business is conducted, goods are made, stored, processed or where services are rendered. It often represents the image of a company.

(3) The events, situations and factors that occur within an organization and influence the behavior of the employees in either positive or negative way. These factors include the company's mission statement, leadership styles and the company's culture.

(4) A group of executives who are responsible for monitoring the activities of the firm's president and other high-level managers.

(5) For most companies, many managerial duties are delegated to other managers.

(6) The responsibility of this department is to purchase goods or services to accomplish the goals of the organization.

(7) A department that is responsible for all of the monetary aspects of a company, from handling credit accounts to compiling information of the tax bureau. It should ensure that there is money for day-to-day operations and oversee investments strategies for future growth.

(8) This department studies the market and the target customers, decides the best way to reach these customers, and works with the rest of the company to help determine the new product needs of the market.

(9) A department of a company which deals with nonpersonal presentation through media or nonmedia forms to influence a large number of consumers. It is a common method for promoting products and services. While advertising is generally more expensive than other methods, it can reach many customers.

(10) The task of this department refers to the effort required to create a new product. It includes the exploration phase that determines the viability of the project and methods for proceeding as well as all the design and manufacturing stages required to yield a working product.

2. Listen to the conversations and answer the questions.

(1) Is Speaker B positive to the cooperation? Why?

(2) What is Nicole Bryant's purpose of the visit?

(3) What is Mr. Jones' purpose of visiting the company?

(4) What business are they talking about?

(5) What does Ms. Oliver want to do?

(6) What is the Addison's opinion of the products?

Part B
Reading

Business Organization

[1] A business may be privately owned in three important forms: the sole proprietorship, the partnership and the corporation. The sole proprietorship is the most common in American business. More than 80 percent of all businesses in the United States are sole proprietorships.

Sole proprietorship

[2] Sole proprietorships, however, do not do the greatest volume of business. They *account for* less than 16 percent of all business *receipts*. What kind of businesses is likely to be a sole proprietorship? These small businesses are very often service industries such as laundromats, beauty shops, repair shops and restaurants.

Partnership

[3] A partnership is an association of two or more persons to carry on a business for profit. When the owners of a partnership have unlimited *liability*, they are called general partners. If one or more partners have limited liability, they are called limited partners. There may be a *silent partner* as well. It is a person who is known to the public as a member of the firm but has no authority in management. There is also the secret partner. It is a person who takes part in management but who is not known to the public.

[4] Any business may be operated as a partnership. There are *partnerships* in *professional* fields such as medicine, law, accounting, insurance and *stockbrokerage*. Limited partnerships are a common form of ownership in *real estate*, *oil prospecting*, and mining and *quarrying* industries, to name a few.

[5] Partnerships are better than sole proprietorships if one needs many sources of capital or *diversified* management. Like sole proprietorships, they are easy to form, and often receive favored treatment by the government as well as tax benefits.

[6] There are a number of disadvantages to partnerships. One is unlimited liability. This means that each partner is responsible for all debts and legal responsibilities in connection with the business. Another disadvantage is that partners may disagree with each other. Problems can also arise with the death of a partner. For example, a share of the business could come into the hands of a less desirable associate.

Corporation

[7] The *privately* owned business *corporation* is an institution established for the purpose of making a profit. It is operated by individuals, whose shares of ownership are represented by stock certificates. Persons owning stock certificates are stockholders.

[8] The corporate form of ownership has several advantages. The first is its ability to attract financial resources. A second advantage is that if the corporation attracts a large amount of capital, it can make large investments in plants, equipment and research. A third advantage is that a corporation can offer high salaries and thus attract talented managers.

[9] The privately owned business corporation is not only the type of corporation that exists. Educational, religious and *charitable* institutions are also permitted to incorporate.

Usually this type of corporation does not issue stock and is a nonprofit institution. If there is a profit, it is generally reinvested in the institution rather than ***distributed*** to private stockholders.

[10] In addition, there are governmental corporations in the United States, which may be established by cities, states, the federal government and special agencies. Some examples of these governmental corporations are state universities, state hospitals and state-owned utilities. Governmental corporations are always nonprofit and usually do not issue stock certificates.

New words and expressions

charitable	['tʃærətəbl]	*adj.*	慈善事业的
corporation	[ˌkɔːpə'reɪʃn]	*n.*	公司；法人（团体）；社团
distributed	[dɪ'strɪbjʊtɪd]	*adj.*	分布式的，分散式的
diversified	[daɪ'vɜːsɪfaɪd]	*adj.*	多样化的；各种的
laundromat	['lɔːndrəʊmæt]	*n.*	（美）自助洗衣店
liability	[laɪə'bɪlətɪ]	*n.*	责任；债务；倾向；可能性；不利因素
partnership	['pɑːtnəʃɪp]	*n.*	合伙；【经管】合伙企业；合作关系
privately	['praɪvɪtlɪ]	*adv.*	私有地，私营地
professional	[prə'feʃənl]	*adj.*	专业的；职业的；职业性的
proprietorship	[prə'praɪətəˌʃɪp]	*n.*	所有权
quarrying	['kwɒrɪɪŋ]	*n.*	采石
receipt	[rɪ'siːt]	*n.*	发票；（企业、银行、政府的）收款，进款；收入
stockbrokerage	['stɒkˌbrəʊkərɪdʒ]	*n.*	证券交易；股票经纪商的业务
utility	[juː'tɪlətɪ]	*n.*	公共设施
account for			共计达；（在数量、比例上）占
oil prospecting			石油勘探
real estate			不动产，房地产
silent partner			隐名合伙人；匿名股东
sole proprietorship			独资企业，独资经营公司

Reading comprehension

1. Work in pairs and discuss the following questions according to the passage.

   (1) Are there different kinds of business ownership? What are they?

   (2) What businesses are often owned in the form of a sole proprietorship?

   (3) What is a silent partner?

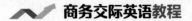

(4) What businesses are likely to be operated as a partnership? And what are the advantages and disadvantages of this form?

(5) What kinds of businesses will be owned the corporate form? And what are the advantages?

2. **Choose the best word or phrase to fill in each blank.**

(1) She has _____ herself as the leading candidate in the firm.
   A. setting up   **B.** set up   C. establishing   D. established

(2) The company _____ a statement about its plan to the public.
   A. issued   **B.** issues   C. declared   D. declares

(3) We are now _____ your company the chance to discount prices at 10%.
   A. accessing   **B.** offering   C. giving   D. presenting

(4) The wealth is not equally _____ among the different businesses.
   A. shared   **B.** owned   C. contributed   D. distributated

(5) There were some hard questions _____ from the Board meeting yesterday.
   A. arising   **B.** causing   C. happening   D. separating

(6) The Labor Union officials _____ the workers will negotiate with the management.
   A. presenting   **B.** presented   C. representing   D. represented

(7) This color is less _____ among young people aged 18 to 25.
   A. welcomed   **B.** wanted   C. needed   D. desirable

(8) The US government is trying to _____ manufacturing industry to America.
   A. make   **B.** transfer   C. attract   D. shift

(9) This new machine _____ several new features in addition to the old one.
   A. covers   **B.** supports   C. benefits   D. incorporates

(10) The close _____ of the president denied the message that he will resign from the office.
   A. association   **B.** associate   C. associated   D. associating

Part C
Listening

Listen to the recording. Decide whether the following statements are True (T) or False (F).

(1) Joe Moreno left Apple because he did not like the company.

(2) In Joe's opinion, Apple Online Store was a profitable project.

(3) Joe did not find anything undesirable working at Apple.

(4) To some extent, Apple's strong competitiveness in the market is due to its policy—secrecy.

(5) Apple workers like to eat at Caffe Macs because of the food and the opportunity to see the top executives.

New words and expressions

administration	[ədˌmɪnɪ'streɪʃn]	*n.*	管理，行政
blog	[blɒg]	*n.*	博客，网络日志
comparable	['kɒmpərəbl]	*adj.*	比得上的，可比较的
compartmentalization	['kɒmpɑːtˌmentəlaɪ'zeɪʃən]	*n.*	知识局限性（尤指军事或科学发展方面）
database	['deɪtəbeɪs]	*n.*	数据库，资料库
dent	[dent]	*n.*	（有效）进展
fandom	['fændəm]	*n.*	［总称］（科幻小说、电影等的）狂热爱好者
highlight	['haɪlaɪt]	*n.*	最精彩的部分，最重要的事情
inbound	['ɪnbaʊnd]	*adj.*	开向本国（或原地）的
infect	[ɪn'fekt]	*vt.*	感染，传染
onslaught	['ɒnslɔːt]	*n.*	冲击，（尤指）猛攻
pasta	['pæstə]	*n.*	面团，意大利面食
revenue	['revənjuː]	*n.*	收入，收益
suite	[swiːt]	*n.*	一套，一组
sushi	['suːʃɪ]	*n.*	寿司（生鱼片冷饭团）
ultra-competitive	['ʌltrə-kəm'petətɪv]	*adj.*	激烈竞争的
consulting division			咨询部
frown upon			表示不赞成
in reference to…			关于
keynote speech			主题演讲

less-than-ideal	不那么理想的
pay issue	薪水问题
WebObjects (Web application)	2003 年苹果公司开发的一种应用软件

Part D
Translating

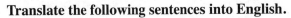

Translate the following sentences into English.

(1) 独资企业的一个主要缺点是，如果生意不成功，你要为所有的损失负责。

(2) 合伙关系比较容易建立，也能为企业带来更多的技能、知识和资本。

(3) 私有合伙企业是以营利为目的而建立的机构。

(4) 企业所有者选择将企业注册为有限责任公司，其主要原因是使自己及其合伙人或投资者承担有限责任。

(5) 从获得资本的多元渠道以及多变的管理模式角度来看，合作经营企业优于独资企业。

Part E
Writing skills: E-mail

写作提示

　　电子邮件（Electronic mail，简称 E-mail）又称电子函件，是一种用电子信息的手段提供信息交换的通信方式。它的最大特点是快速、方便、经济、可靠。

　　电子邮件可以分为正式和非正式两种形式。公函为正式电子邮件，私函一般属于非正式邮件。常用的公函有公务来往信函、推荐信和通告等。私函主要用于私人之间的信件往来。正式的电子邮件一般包括收件人、发件人、主题、称呼、开头语、正文、结尾语、署名几个部分。在实际工作和生活中，可以根据情况有所减少。

　　写电子邮件跟传统商务信函一样，需要根据收件人的特点采用适当的措辞技巧，同时也要遵守互联网的礼节和规范，避免产生误会。

　　首先，电子邮件的内容应该简明扼要，句子、段落必须简洁，以一意为一段。其次，要提供主题，把邮件内容的概要写到主题中，便于收件人了解邮件内容，提高工作效率。第三，把最重要的信息放在最前面，信息的主体内容要完整、清晰，让收件人快速、准确地了解相关信息。第四，所有信息要一次提供给收件人，同时直接提出问题，使收件人清楚你的意图，不要让收件人去猜测。第五，用词准确，有理有节，诚恳动人，通常使用普通、简单的词，避免出现语法、标点符号、数字、拼写等方面的错误，所有信息必须准确无误。

Example

From: Jane Smith <jane_smith@martketingabc.com>

To: <john_lee@cde.com>

Subject: Thanks for reaching out to us John!

Hi John,

Thank you for reaching out to learn more about Marketing ABC! The best way to learn about our offerings as they pertain to your particular business is to set up a free marketing consultation with one of our specialists. During the one-hour session, we will assess your online presence and then identify which of our products and/or services are best suited for your business.

There will be no obligation to sign up afterward, and will also provide easy-to-implement tips throughout the call that you can do on your own.

If you'd like to set up one of these super helpful consultations, click here to choose a time slot or just give us a call at (617)555-7117.

We look forward to hearing from you!

Best regards.

Jane Smith

Director of Client Services

Marketing ABC

(617)555-7117

marketingabc.com

Case writing

Task: You work for the Purchase Department of Jiangnan Machinery Company. Your department ordered 3,000 GT79 gears from IC Industries Company. When the goods arrived, you found that the gears were GT97, and there were only 2,000 gears.

Write an e-mail to Mr. Smith, the Sale Manager of IC Industry Company:

* to point out the mistakes;
* to request action;
* to give a warning.

Write in about **120-140** words.

Part F
Further business story

What Is Organizational Culture

Organizational culture **encompasses** values and behaviours that contribute to the unique social and **psychological** environment of an organization. According to Needle (2004), organizational culture represents the collective values, beliefs and principles of organizational members and is a product of such factors as history, product, market, technology, strategy, type of employees, management style, and national culture; culture includes the organization's vision, values, norms, systems, symbols, language, assumptions, beliefs, and habits.

Organizational culture is a common phrase that one encounters in the business world. Organizational culture is not tangible. It can be best understood by studying the behavior, the attitudes, the values and belief system of the employees. It characterizes and colors our **perception** of the business entity. Any employee however efficient will be a **misfit** if he is unable to adapt himself to the work culture. Organizations are laying emphasis on culture since growth and success depends on the kind of culture **prevalent** in the company. Do employees feel threatened or cherished? Is there a desire to work and grow? Do they want to evolve as a group or go their separate ways? These questions can be answered by a careful examination of the organizational culture.

Organizational behavior

Organizational culture and behavior are quite **interrelated** as organizational culture influences behavior and **vice-versa**. Organizational behavior is the study of how individuals behave in an organization. It is one of the key areas in the field of management. Organizational behavior, as the name suggests, studies the behaviors of individuals but is **restricted** to the behaviors displayed by them in the organization. It deals with the overt and covert behaviors of employees and their response to certain **stimuli**. It also studies an important branch of group and team **dynamics**. The point of studying organizational behavior by managers is to understand the behaviors of employees, why they behave in a particular way, and look for ways in which wrong employee behaviors can be improved.

Over the years several organizational behavior theories have been suggested. These theories give the various models of organizational systems. Organizational systems have been *modified* over time to ensure employee satisfaction and organizational progress. Organizational behavior is the art and science which advocates that there can indeed be mutual satisfaction between employees and the management as opposed to the old *notion* that these two parties are always at loggerheads due to *disparate* visions. Organizational behavior says that a shared vision and employee motivation leads an organization towards success.

This was all about organizational culture and behavior. It is interesting to know that organizational culture is a part of the vast topic of organizational behavior. After all, organizational culture too deals with the *modification* and improvement in organizational behavior of individuals.

Strong culture

Strong culture is said to exist where staff respond to stimulus because of their *alignment* to organizational values. In such environments, strong cultures help firms operate like well-oiled machines, engaging in outstanding execution with only minor adjustments to existing procedures as needed.

Research shows that organizations that foster strong cultures have clear values that give employees a reason to embrace the culture. A "strong" culture may be especially beneficial to firms operating in the service sector since members of these organizations are responsible for delivering the service and for evaluations important constituents make about firms. Organizations may derive the following benefits from developing strong and productive cultures:

- better aligning the company towards achieving its vision, mission, and goals;
- high employee *motivation* and loyalty;
- increased team cohesiveness among the company's various departments and divisions;
- promoting consistency and encouraging coordination and control within the company;
- shaping employee behavior at work, enabling the organization to be more efficient.

New words and expressions

alignment   *n.*   （力量的）组合；联合，结盟

disparate	*adj.*	全异的；不同的
dynamics	*n.*	动力，活力
encompass	*vt.*	包含
interrelated	*adj.*	相关的；互相联系的
misfit	*n.*	不适合；不适应环境的人
modification	*n.*	修改，修正；改变
modify	*vt.*	更改，修改
motivation	*n.*	动机；推动；积极性
notion	*n.*	概念；见解
perception	*n.*	认识；观念；看法
prevalent	*adj.*	流行的，普遍的，广传的
psychological	*adj.*	心理的；心理学的；精神上的
restrict	*vt.*	限制，限定；约束
stimuli	*n.*	刺激；刺激物；促进因素（stimulus 的复数）
vice-versa		反之亦然

Critical thinking

Work in groups and discuss the following questions.

(1) What is the organizational culture?

(2) How are organizational culture and organizational behavior interrelated?

(3) What are the advantages and disadvantages for organizations to develop strong culture?

Unit 4
Working Patterns

In recent decades, the labor market has witnessed anti-discrimination legislation, labor market deregulation, and enterprise bargaining. These developments have been accompanied by changes in the composition of the workforce and increased diversity of working arrangements and patterns. Gradually teamwork and flexible working patterns begin to arouse people's interest for where there are people, there is teamwork.

Learning objectives

* To familiarize with the words and expressions about team building;
* To discuss the secrets of great teamwork;
* To extract the main ideas from a listening text about effective teams;
* To understand the structure of a letter of complaint.

Warm-up questions

(1) What do you know about working patterns?

(2) Is teamwork really important in business world? Why or why not?

Part A
General business vocabulary

1. Match the words in the box with the following descriptions.

> A. dysfunction   B. consensus   C. autonomy   D. climate
> E. groupthink   F. dynamic   G. norm   H. fundamental

(1) A place or an organization has freedom to govern or control itself.

(2) It is an opinion that everyone in a group agrees with or accepts.

(3) It is the basic rule or principle of something.

(4) The set of forces exists in a situation, especially a relationship, and affect how it changes or develops.

(5) It refers to the usual and expected situation, way of doing something, etc.

(6) The interpersonal behavior or interaction within a group is abnormal or unhealthy.

(7) It is related to the general feeling or situation in a place at a particular time.

(8) A pattern of thought is characterized by self-deception, forced manufacture of consent, and conformity to group values and ethics.

2. Listen to the conversations and answer the questions.

(1) What are they talking about?

(2) What does the second speaker study?

(3) What is the first speaker's opinion about teamwork?

(4) What is critically important to the team's ultimate success?

(5) What is the corporate culture of the second speaker's new company?

(6) What kind of attitude does the second speaker have towards his or her new boss?

(7) What is the second speaker's idea of a leader's role?

(8) What are the two speakers' ideas of delegation?

Part B
Reading

The Secrets of Great Teamwork

[1] Today's teams are different from the teams of the past: They're far more diverse, *dispersed*, digital, and *dynamic* (with frequent changes in membership). But while teams face new *hurdles*, their success still *hinges on* a core set of *fundamentals* for group *collaboration*.

[2] The basics of team effectiveness were identified by J. Richard Hackman, a pioneer in the field of organizational behavior. In more than 40 years of his research, he uncovered a *groundbreaking* insight: What teams need to thrive are a compelling direction, a strong structure, and a supportive context. In fact, today those three requirements demand more attention than ever. But we've also seen that modern teams are *vulnerable* to certain *corrosive* problems. To overcoming those *pitfalls* requires a fourth critical condition: a shared mindset.

[3] Let's explore in greater detail how to create a climate that helps diverse, dispersed, digital, dynamic teams—what we like to call 4D teams—attain high performance.

Compelling direction

[4] The foundation of every great team is a direction that energizes, orients, and engages its members. Teams cannot be inspired if they don't know what they're working toward and don't have *explicit* goals. Those goals should be challenging (modest ones don't motivate) but not so difficult that the team becomes *dispirited*. They also must be *consequential*: People have to care about achieving a goal, whether because they stand to gain extrinsic rewards, like recognition, pay, and promotions, or intrinsic rewards, such as satisfaction and a sense of meaning.

[5] On 4D teams, direction is especially crucial because it's easy for *far-flung* members from *dissimilar* backgrounds to hold different views of the group's purpose. Solving the difference between members required a frank discussion to reach *consensus* on how the team as a whole defined its objectives.

Strong structure

[6] Teams also need the right mix and number of members, optimally designed tasks and processes, and norms that discourage destructive behavior and promote positive dynamics.

[7] High-performing teams include members with a balance of skills. Every individual doesn't have to possess *superlative* technical and social skills, but the team overall needs a healthy dose of both. Diversity in knowledge, views, and perspectives, as well as in age, gender, and race can help teams be more creative and avoid *groupthink*.

[8] Adding members is of course one way to ensure that a team has the requisite skills and diversity, but increased size comes with costs. Team leaders must be *vigilant* about adding members only when necessary.

[9] Team assignments should be designed with equal care. Not every task has to be highly creative or inspiring; many require a certain amount of *drudgery*. But leaders can make any task more motivating by ensuring that the team is responsible for a significant piece of work from beginning to end, that the team members have a lot of *autonomy* in managing that work, and that the team receives performance feedback on it.

[10] Destructive dynamics can undermine collaborative efforts. Team members withhold information, pressure people to conform, avoid responsibility, cast blame, and so on. Teams can reduce the potential for *dysfunction* by establishing clear norms—rules that spell out a small number of things members must always do and a small number they must never do.

Supportive context

[11] Having the right support is the third condition that enables team effectiveness. This includes maintaining a reward system that reinforces good performance, an information system that provides access to the data needed for the work, and an educational system that offers training, and last—but not least—securing the material resources required to do the job, such as funding and technological assistance. While no team ever gets everything it wants, leaders can head off a lot of problems by taking the time to get the essential pieces in place from the start.

[12] Ensuring a supportive context is often difficult for teams that are geographically distributed and digitally dependent, because the resources available to members may vary a lot.

Shared mindset

[13] Establishing the first three enabling conditions will pave the way for team success, as Hackman and his colleagues showed. But today's teams need something more. Distance and diversity, as well as digital communication and changing membership, make them

especially prone to some problems. The solution is developing a shared mindset among team members—something team leaders can do by fostering a common identity and common understanding.

[14] In the past teams typically consisted of a stable set of fairly *homogeneous* members who worked face-to-face and tended to have a similar mindset. But that's no longer the case, and teams now often perceive themselves not as one *cohesive* group but as several smaller subgroups. But we also are inclined to view our own subgroup—whether it's our function, our unit, our region, or our culture—more positively than others, and that habit often creates tension and hinders collaboration.

[15] Fortunately, there are many ways team leaders can actively foster a shared identity and shared understanding and break down the barriers to cooperation and information exchange. One powerful approach is to ensure that each subgroup feels valued for its contributions toward the team's overall goals.

[16] You can prime teams for success by focusing on the four fundamentals.

New words and expressions

autonomy	[ɔː'tɒnəmɪ]	*n.*	自治，自治权
cohesive	[kəʊ'hiːsɪv]	*adj.*	凝聚的；有结合力的
collaboration	[kə,læbə'reɪʃn]	*n.*	合作
consensus	[kən'sensəs]	*n.*	一致
consequential	[,kɒnsɪ'kwenʃl]	*adj.*	结果的；重要的
corrosive	[kə'rəʊsɪv]	*adj.*	腐蚀的；侵蚀性的
dispersed	[dɪ'spɜːst]	*adj.*	散布的；被分散的；被驱散的
dispirited	[dɪ'spɪrɪtɪd]	*adj.*	沮丧的；意气消沉的
dissimilar	[dɪ'sɪmɪlə]	*adj.*	不同的
drudgery	['drʌdʒərɪ]	*n.*	苦工，苦差事
dynamic	[daɪ'næmɪk]	*adj.*	有活力的 *n.* 动力
dysfunction	[dɪs'fʌŋkʃn]	*n.*	功能紊乱；机能障碍
explicit	[ɪk'splɪsɪt]	*adj.*	明确的；清楚的
far-flung	['fɑː'flʌŋ]	*adj.*	广泛的；广布的
fundamental	[,fʌndə'mentl]	*n.*	基本原理；基本原则
groundbreaking	['graʊndbreɪkɪŋ]	*adj.*	开创性的
groupthink	['gruːpθɪŋk]	*n.*	集体审议
homogeneous	[,hɒmə(ʊ)'dʒiːnɪəs]	*adj.*	同种的；同类的
hurdle	['hɜːdl]	*n.*	障碍
pitfall	['pɪtfɔːl]	*n.*	缺陷
superlative	[suː'pɜːlətɪv]	*adj.*	最高级的

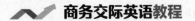
vigilant	['vɪdʒɪl(ə)nt]	*adj.*	注意的
vulnerable	['vʌlnərəbl]	*adj.*	易受攻击的
hinge on			取决于……

Reading comprehension

1. Work in pairs and discuss the following questions according to the passage.

    (1) What are the secrets of teamwork?

    (2) Why should team leaders set goals for teams?

    (3) How should team leaders arrange team assignments for teams?

    (4) What should a team leader do to maintain a team's effectiveness?

    (5) Why do team leaders need the fourth condition?

2. Choose the best answers to explain the meanings of the underlined words.

    (1) Instead of remaining concentrated at the surface, <u>dispersed</u> oil pollutes the entire water column.

        A. disappointed   **B.** concentrated   **C.** disagreeable   **D.** distributed

    (2) The only explanation for their <u>groundbreaking</u> victory is the impact of their inspiring culture.

        A. sparse   **B.** connected   **C.** innovative   **D.** satisfying

    (3) Having people motivated by <u>extrinsic</u> goals (money) is a very bad way to run knowledge-based organizations.

        A. extra   **B.** external   **C.** internal   **D.** exact

    (4) No matter how well its transmissions are encoded, the device itself remains <u>vulnerable</u> to being hacked.

        A. unprotected   **B.** exaggerated   **C.** coherent   **D.** articulated

    (5) Their behavior became more and more collective as signals became more and more <u>explicit</u>.

        A. exclusive   **B.** organic   **C.** definite   **D.** responsive

    (6) The continued speculation and uncertainty is allowing our opponents to portray us as <u>dispirited</u> and disunited.

        A. lively   **B.** spiritless   **C.** authoritative   **D.** daring

    (7) What makes these points so <u>consequential</u> is the unique math of the United States Senate.

        A. sequential   **B.** objective   **C.** sufficient   **D.** important

    (8) Companies are also becoming more <u>vigilant</u>, as their employees have been implicated in insider-trading cases.

        A. alert   **B.** temporary   **C.** resistant   **D.** predictable

(9) He was fascinated by the <u>dynamics</u> of change and innovation in the market.

    A. images   **B.** obligations   **C.** digestions   **D.** incentives

(10) The <u>diversity</u> of the collection ranges from photographs, patient letters, admission certificates and application forms.

    A. cultivation   **B.** revolution   **C.** variety   **D.** privilege

Part C
Listening

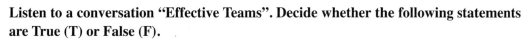

Listen to a conversation "Effective Teams". Decide whether the following statements are True (T) or False (F).

(1) In Glenn Parker's book, he just provided general and theoretical tools to help business leaders and team members.

(2) From Parker's point of view, teams quickly became part of the culture at many well-known companies.

(3) Parker never tried to force himself to develop his creative abilities.

(4) When teams have various approaches to problem-solving, decision-making, communication, conflict resolution, and critical thinking, more creative ideas are the result.

(5) People are at their best when the atmosphere around them is informal and relaxed.

New words and expressions

antithesis	[æn'tɪθəsɪs]	*n.*	对照
breakthrough	['breɪkθruː]	*n.*	突破；突破性进展
censure	['senʃə]	*n.*	责难
clash	[klæʃ]	*n.*	冲突
compliment	['kɒmplɪmənt]	*vt.*	称赞
distinctly	[dɪ'stɪŋktlɪ]	*adv.*	明显地
fad	[fæd]	*n.*	一时的爱好；一时流行的狂热
gimmick	['gɪmɪk]	*n.*	骗人的玩意；花招
hallmark	['hɔːlmɑːk]	*n.*	特点

hands-on	[ˌhændzˈɒn]	*adj.*	亲身实践的，亲自动手的
pharmaceutical	[ˌfɑːməˈsuːtɪkl]	*adj.*	制药（学）的
		n.	药物
ridicule	[ˈrɪdɪkjuːl]	*n.*	嘲笑
Xerox	[ˈzɪrɑks]	*n.*	施乐。施乐 (Xerox) 是美国施乐公司一个著名商标和品牌。施乐公司于 1906 年成立于美国康涅狄格州费尔菲尔德。作为商标，"施乐"只用来标识施乐公司的各种产品和服务，如施乐复印机、施乐打印机等。
quick fix			权宜之计
3M			3M 公司。该公司是一家历史悠久的多元化跨国企业，其开发生产的优质产品多达 5 万种，公司业务包括通信、交通、工业、汽车、航天、航空、电子、电气、医疗、建筑、文教办公及日用消费等诸多领域。

Part D
Translating

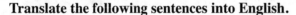

Translate the following sentences into English.

(1) 团队成员之间的关系建立在相互信任和尊重的基础上。

(2) 今天的团队不同于过去的团队，他们更多样化，更分散，更具流动性。

(3) 团队发展壮大需要一个激发兴趣的方向、一个强大的组织、一个支持的环境和一种共享的心态。

(4) 增加成员是一种确保团队拥有必要技能和保持多样性的一种方法，但团队规模增加伴随着成本上升。

(5) 如果没有具体的绩效目标，团队成员就会对他们的贡献缺乏清晰的认识，因而表现平庸。

(6) 这个基于团队的方法会提高组织的效率和生产力水平。

Part E
Writing skills: Letter of complaint

写作提示

投诉信(Letter of complaint)在生活中很常见，目的是获取更好的服务，对已出现的问题求得尽快、妥善解决。在商务往来中，它通常是买方由于对收到的货物不满或是服务不合理而书写。

书写投诉信有以下事项需要注意：第一，投诉信应该简洁，及时；第二，信件的内容需要明确，清楚；第三，强调解决方法和赔偿；第四，如果有若干点要提及，最好依次按照顺序列举；第五，避免愤怒和使对方过于难堪的措辞。

写投诉信的时候，如果涉及合同号，需要在主题行标明。在投诉信的开篇，一定写清楚投诉的原因并提供确实的证据，如货物未按时到达，货物有损毁现象，货物数量短缺或多余，服务不合理以及收费过高等。写投诉信的时候还要说明确切的时间、地点、人物、说过的话或做过的事。通过投诉信期望得到什么反馈和怎样的赔偿可以在信函结尾处提及。

Example

Dear Mr. Smith,

Would you immediately replace the visual software for W5060 with that for W5065 which we have paid for?

On July 2, we purchased the communication system W5065 from your sales representative Peter Anderson. As your file may show, we paid $3,900 for it, which is $100 more expensive than W5060. That payment includes free installment and a six-month trial period.

The software we bought operated well at first, but the system refused to work after three weeks. After careful examination, we found what you sent us is W5060, not W5065 we purchased.

I communicated with Mr. Anderson on July 28. He said he was out on business in another city. He promised to arrange a technician to replace it. Four days has passed, but nothing happened.

It is urgent that you send people to replace the software and install the system again. The collapse of the system has caused serious problems to our normal work. The replacement is expected no later than July 30.

Please call me at 021-47103268 any time before 4:00 pm. I am confident that you are serious about the matter. If I haven't received your call by 10:00 this Thursday, I will reluctantly turn this issue to my lawyer for actions against you.

We appreciate your prompt action.

Sincerely yours,

Bob Jackson

Case writing

Task: Write a complaint letter based on the following directions.

* You are Kelly Smith; you and your friends went to a coffee shop and received impolite treatment last Sunday evening.

* Write a letter to someone who is possibly in charge, describing your experience on that night and expressing your dissatisfaction.

Write in **120-140** words.

Part F

Further business story

Two Car Companies, One Challenge

How complementary skills and resources can multiply results beyond the wildest expectations.

Henry Ford's assembly line would never happened without help. Although history tends to favor the lone-wolf entrepreneur, it's usually teams that actually get the job done.

Says Tricia Naddaff, president of Management Research Group, a leadership specialist: "When teams interact, they create a new, stronger entity. There's nothing better than a new and enthusiastic team that, on a ***shoestring budget***, tries to do something that's never been done before. They have to be ***agile***, to deal with complexity, to stay centered when everything goes to hell—and they have to be able to pull everything together anyway." The following two car companies are concrete examples.

The ***quandary*** for Ford and Chevrolet: How to update and improve automotive icons—the F-150 ***pickup truck*** and the ***hybrid*** Volt, respectively—without eroding the qualities that made them popular.

Ford ***was poised to*** take a huge gamble. Its F-150 pickup truck is the best-selling vehicle in the country and has been for more than 30 years. But Ford wanted better fuel efficiency for 2015, which meant introducing economical six-*cylinder* EcoBoost engines and—far more radical—using an all-aluminum body. Would consumers accept the change?

The F-150 team began planning a year and a half before the program kickoff, asking, "What is the marketplace going to say to a truck with a body made of high-strength aluminum?" Trucks are available in a bewildering number of versions, and all had to be shaped to take advantage of the coming weight savings.

Pete Reyes was chief engineer for the all-important—and top-secret—F-150 project. He agrees that planning a new vehicle is like producing a movie. "Your team *conceives* it, hammers it out, and hopefully it goes on to a long and prosperous production run," Reyes says. "We had all these parallel work teams on different aspects of the truck, and we'd meet once a month for 18 months, making sure all the work would come together into a viable vehicle. Everybody crossed boundaries, and they came back with a lot of feedback that shaped what we were going to do."

The F-150 team that handled the *nitty-gritty* of building the new truck included Peter Frantzeskakis, Ford F-150 development manager, and Jerry Farrell, the chief program manager. The three of them are unbelievable workhorses, and they each could have done the other's job. Whether it was marketing or manufacturing, we stuck with common goals.

The 1,000-member team encountered unique problems, such as the fact that the world's existing supply of high-strength, auto-grade aluminum wasn't enough to cover the F-150's volume. "We had to build that supply," Reyes says.

The switch to aluminum was central to the truck's 700-pound weight loss, but the team's other innovations contributed considerably: 70 pounds came out of the steel frame, 23 pounds out of the steering *knuckles*, 26.9 out of the mechanical emergency brake, 31.7 from the front seats and 2.7 pounds from the *front bumper* structure. *Fuel economy* increased as much as 29 percent, depending on model.

And the marketplace reaction? In October 2015, Ford announced third-quarter earnings of $1.9 billion, up $1.1 billion, from 2014 largely on strong sales of the new F-150.

Chevrolet's challenge, meanwhile, was to build a second-generation Volt *plug-in* hybrid car, satisfying consumers' requests for more electric range and better interior space without *ditching* the vehicle's user-friendly profile. GM needed a team of more than 500—about half the size of Ford's—working to update the Volt, which isn't the sales *juggernaut* of the F-150.

Andrew Farah was the chief engineer on the 2016 Volt. "Our team set the goal of 50-mile electric range for the Volt, and in the end we reached 53," Farah says. "Our team was similar to others within GM, but if you talked to my people they'd say it was run a bit differently. It was less about authority and more about cooperating and figuring out how to take on risk."

Auto teams are usually highly risk-*averse*, but the Volt—as GM's groundbreaking electric vehicle with relatively low production numbers—allows exceptions. The vehicle itself is inherently risky ("Taking moderate risks" is a characteristic of successful management teams, according to Venture Founders Corp.), and *revamping* it was subject to different rules. "We could afford to take on more risk than if we were working on a bread-and-butter *sedan* or midsized SUV," Farah says. "Our volumes are much lower, frankly. We have only one assembly plant and a smaller set of suppliers who can respond quickly. If we have to spend an extra 10 cents on a part, it's not that big a deal."

The Volt team worked closely together, and members had less rigid roles than is usual in GM's corporate culture. "Everyone came to understand the appropriate amount of risk and accept the plan." Farah says. We could bend a rule or two. We could work quickly, skipping some of the usual steps, as long as we kept asking ourselves. Is the view worth the climb?

The Volt team's *mantra* evolved in ambition, first being "Gen 1 or better" and then becoming "Gen 2, better in every way." The car now has 50-plus miles of electric-only range, a lighter battery pack that nonetheless stores 20 percent more energy, and better-communicating electric motors that deliver 20 percent better low-speed acceleration. And the back seat can hold three people, not just two.

The *makeover* also benefited from the fresh thinking of new recruits: smart young engineers who had just competed in college contests such as the EcoCAR and Challenge X. In these years-long competitions co-sponsored by automakers, passionate students often stay up all night with pizza and laptops to finish building electric and *fuel-cell* cars. In one year, GM hired 55 Challenge X graduates, mostly to work on the electric and hybrid cars that the recruits were already passionate about.

Incidentally, the redesigned F-150 and Volt were named the green truck and green car of the year at the Los Angeles and San Antonio auto shows in late November.

New words and expressions

agile	*adj.*	机敏的
averse	*adj.*	反对的；不愿意的
conceive	*vt.*	构思
cylinder	*n.*	汽缸
ditch	*vt.*	丢弃
fuel-cell	*n.*	燃料电池

hybrid	*adj.*	混合的
juggernaut	*n.*	强大的破坏力
knuckle	*n.*	转向节
makeover	*n.*	大转变
mantra	*n.*	颂歌
nitty-gritty	*n.*	事实真相；本质
plug-in	*n.*	插件程序，插件法
quandary	*n.*	窘境
revamp	*vt.*	修改
sedan	*n.*	轿车
be poised to		随时准备着
front bumper		前保险杠；前车挡
fuel economy		节约燃料
pickup truck		敞篷小型载货卡车
shoestring budget		紧缩的预算

Critical thinking

Work in groups and discuss the following questions.

(1) If you are a leader of a group, what will you do to improve the cooperation among the members?

(2) As a team leader, how will you allocate assignment to your team members to arouse their motivation and interest?

(3) Supposing that you're a leader of a group, what will you do to prevent yourself from falling behind?

Unit 5
Business Meeting

A meeting is a group of people who are gathered for a shared purpose. Business meetings and conferences play a very important part in business world. Most business people must come in contact with colleagues from both inside and outside the organization, and with both subordinates and superiors, formally and informally. Communication must be exchanged and information transmitted. And at the time, meetings are an important aspect of business organization. The most important are statutory meeting, annual general meeting, extraordinary general meeting, board meeting and committee meeting.

Learning objectives

* To explain the basic terms or concepts on business meeting;
* To grasp the skills of conducting a meeting;
* To identify the details of a listening text about a business meeting;
* To grasp the tips of minutes writing.

Warm-up questions

(1) What are the purposes of business meetings?

(2) How to prepare a business meeting?

Part A
General business vocabulary

1. **Match the words or phrases in the box with the following descriptions.**

A. agenda   B. amendment   C. motion

D. second a motion   E. adjourn   F. rising vote

G. voice vote   H. secret ballot   I. minute   J. chairperson

(1) It is a formal or official change made to a law, contract, constitution, or other legal document.

(2) It is an indication that there is at least one person besides the mover that is interested in seeing the motion come before the meeting. It does not necessarily indicate that the seconder favors the motion.

(3) It is a formal proposal by a member of the meeting to do something. These proposals are the basis of the group decision-making process.

(4) It refers to points to be discussed, sometimes refers to the list of topics itself.

(5) It means to end something (such as a meeting or session) for a period of time.

(6) It refers to a voting method in which members stand and are counted for their choice.

(7) That is someone who presides over a meeting, board, etc.

(8) It refers to a voting method in which a voter's choices in a meeting or an election are anonymous, forestalling attempts to influence the voter by intimidation and potential vote buying.

(9) It refers to a written record (usually formal) of a meeting.

(10) It refers to a voting method in which a vote is taken on a topic or motion by responding verbally.

2. What are the conversations about? Choose one for each of the comersations.

(1) Confirming a meeting (by e-mail)

(2) Working through an agenda

(3) Reaching an agreement

(4) Postponing a meeting (by phone)

(5) Setting up a meeting (by phone)

(6) Making a point

(7) Reporting back to a meeting

(8) Setting up a meeting (by a voicemail message)

Part B
Reading

Types of Corperate Meetings

[1] Every corporation holds an annual meeting of stockholder for the election of directors. During the year, it may also hold other meetings when the stock-holder' *consent* is required for some proposed action, such as an increase or decrease in *capital stock*, an *amendment* of the *corporate charter*, or a *merger*. *Annual stockholder meetings* have special legal requirements for meeting notices must be sent. Printed notices are sent along with *proxy* voting forms and a return address, postal paid envelope. As an *administrative assistant*, your duties include preparing notices of the meeting as well as a proxy form to be used in case a stockholder cannot attend. This proxy gives another person the right to vote for the stockholder. These must be sent to everyone concerned, in accordance with the *bylaws* of the group. In most cases, these notices must be sent out three to four weeks in advance.

[2] You must arrange for a meeting place and *confirm* that it will be ready for use at the time specified. You'll also type and distribute the *agenda*. On the day of the meeting, place all *pertinent* papers in a folder with the *corporate seal* on the conference table at the chairperson's seat.

[3] If you act as the recorder of the meeting, sit beside the chairperson in order to hear every word distinctly. If you have difficulty in hearing, signal the chairperson, who will then ask for a repetition of what has been said. Before the meeting, read all resolutions and reports to be presented. In addition, obtain the list of the persons attending (which you should have from distributing the agenda), and check the *absentees* ahead of time

rather than write down names while the *roll* is being called. The greater your knowledge is of the meeting's purpose and the *attendees*, the easier it will be to record the meeting.

[4] Corporate director meetings are specified by the corporate bylaws. Most companies have quarterly or yearly director meetings. A written notice of these meetings is not required by law. An administrative assistant may be asked to contact directors via phone, letter, or e-mail to inform them of an upcoming meeting. The assistant will also be asked to track who is coming to the meeting and who has declined. A list of those attending the meeting should be created and made available at the meeting. Other corporate meetings that are not regular events should be scheduled two weeks in advance. You should send out an invitation, agenda, and a follow-up reminder. The date, time, location, and subject should be clear in the invitation. Outside meetings and conferences usually require printed invitations sent out as a mass mailing.

[5] Double-check all the information on a proof of the invitation before it is printed. Confirm the date, week, day, time, room, location, and names of all the speakers. No one should have to telephone the *sponsor* to get information that was *inadvertently* omitted from the invitation.

New words and expressions

absentee	[ˌæbsən'tiː]	n.	缺席者
agenda	[ə'dʒendə]	n.	议程
amendment	[ə'mendmənt]	n.	修正，修正案
attendee	[æten'diː]	n.	与会者；参加者
bylaw	['baɪlɔː]	n.	章程；细则
confirm	[kən'fɜːm]	vt.	确认；确定
consent	[kən'sent]	n.	同意；（意见等）一致
inadvertently	[ˌɪnəd'vɜːtəntlɪ]	adv.	非故意地
merger	['mɜːdʒə]	n.	合并
pertinent	['pɜːtɪnənt]	adj.	相关的
proxy	['prɒksɪ]	n.	代理人，委托书
roll	[rəʊl]	n.	名单
sponsor	['spɒnsə]	n.	主办人；主办方
administrative assistant			行政助理
annual stockholder meeting			年度股东大会
capital stock			股本
corporate charter			公司执照；公司注册证
corporate seal			公司印章；法人印章

Reading comprehension

1. **Work in pairs and discuss the following questions according to the passage.**

   (1) What kinds of meetings might a corporation hold?

   (2) What preparations are needed for a meeting?

   (3) What should a recorder do at the meeting?

   (4) How to contact directors to inform them of an upcoming meeting?

   (5) What information should be double-checked before the invitations are printed?

2. **Choose the best answer to fill in each blank.**

   (1) She asked several highly _____ questions.

   A. relation   **B.** relative   **C.** relationship   **D.** pertinent

   (2) Please _____ your telephone message by writing to me.

   A. test   **B.** confirm   **C.** examine   **D.** strengthen

   (3) The critical issue is that your projects have no funds _____.

   A. access   **B.** offer   **C.** available   **D.** avail

   (4) He threw me a smile that telegraphed _____.

   A. admire   **B.** jealous   **C.** complement   **D.** consent

   (5) The press magnate decided on a _____ with another company to expand his empire.

   A. merger   **B.** disinvestment   **C.** dissolution   **D.** separation

   (6) They decided to add a/an _____ to the contract.

   A. item   **B.** terms   **C.** recommend   **D.** amendment

   (7) Two days after the meeting, we received the ballots boxes of the _____.

   A. ballets   **B.** contracts   **C.** absentees   **D.** abstract

   (8) Should college teachers call the _____ in class?

   A. roll   **B.** role   **C.** run   **D.** names

   (9) "All of us together, in that beautiful place," one _____ recalls.

   A. attend   **B.** attendee   **C.** attending   **D.** attention

   (10) Many people _____ transpose digits of the ZIP code.

   A. inadvertently   **B.** prominently   **C.** obviously   **D.** extraordinarily

商务交际英语教程

Part C
Listening

Listen to the recording of a business meeting. Decide whether the following statements are True (T) or False (F).

(1) The meeting will probably last less than two hours.

(2) The minutes of the last meeting was accepted in this meeting.

(3) Three issues will be discussed at the meeting.

(4) The second issue will not be discussed at this meeting because a law expert won't come.

(5) The company business in Africa has grown by leaps and bounds.

(6) They decided to find some reliable foreign distribution firms to deal with the complaints about delivery times.

New words and expressions

minutes	['mɪnɪts]	n.	会议记录
proactive	[prəʊ'æktɪv]	adj.	主动的，先发制人的
reliance	[rɪ'laɪəns]	n.	依赖，依靠
revenue	['revənjuː]	n.	来自财产或投资的收益；收入
stagnancy	['stægnənsɪ]	n.	停滞；迟钝；萧条；不景气
act on			针对情况采取措施
bottle-neck		n.	瓶颈
by leaps and bounds			飞跃性地
call on			邀请；指派；请人回答问题
cast the final approval			对最终议案投票
lay out			布置；安排
motion carried			决议通过
pick up			获得
set in motion			采取行动
stand to do			将会；有某种倾向
take the floor			（在会议上）发言，参加讨论
trend chart			趋势图

Part D
Translating

Translate the following sentences into English.

(1) 团队建设会议可以改善员工之间的工作关系，提高员工对公司的忠诚度。

(2) 参加会议时，着装得体可以显示出对与会者的尊重和专业精神。

(3) 会议纪要可以方便与会者会后回顾会议，了解突出的问题和行动项目。

(4) 会议日程为讨论提供了方向，确保讨论偏离议题时能及时回到正轨上。

(5) 我们这个分部在海外市场才刚起步，我希望能听听各位对于目前和未来计划的看法。

Part E
Writing skills: Minutes

写作提示

无论是员工会议还是有经理、总裁和投资人、员工参加的会议，都需要有人来记录会议内容，并将其公布给未能参会的各方。会议记录对于与会者来说能起到提醒的作用，帮助他们回忆起讨论过的内容、做出的决定和将要采取的行动。会议记录为企业的未来行动指明方向，因此应当具有严谨的结构，包含必要的信息。

会议记录的目的并不是要记下与会者讨论的每一件事，而是要记录发生了什么事情。在记录时，不要试图记下人们针对某一商务行为做出的每一个论点。例如，当有人提出动议时，需要记下这个动议的确切措辞、动议的提出者是谁，和最终的投票结果，但不必记下每一个人对该动议的评论。当有人做报告的时候，需要记录做报告的人是谁、报告的标题，并对报告进行简短地概括，以及采取的行动。会议记录还需要列出决议通过的时间和大家开始讨论的时间。

通常，会议记录可以包括以下内容：

- 会议的时间和地点（time and location of the meeting）
- 参加会议的人员（attendees）
- 上次会议记录（minutes of last meeting）
- 上次会议记录跟进事项（matters arising from the minutes）

- 本次会议的议题（special or new business），包括报告、讨论以及通过的决议等
- 其他事项或例外事件 [any other business (AOB) or usual occurrences]
- 下次会议时间（date of next meeting）
- 休会时间（adjournment time）

会议一结束就应当完成会议记录的草稿，因为这时的记忆非常清楚。会议记录的草稿写好后，要先交由会议主持人过目，做必要的改动，然后再分发给各成员。有的公司有会议记录的模板，可以据此进行记录。

Example

Sally's Bakery Business Meeting

February 9 2020

Meeting called to order at 2:30 pm. by bakery owner Sally Honer.

Employees present:

Ashley Logan, *Manager*

Taylor Cooper, *Assistant Manager*

Abby Morgan, *Associate*

Mark Sellers, *Baker*

Sharon Bess, *Baker*

Members not present:

(none)

Approval of minutes:

Motion: To approve the minutes for January 5 2020

Vote: Motion carried

Resolved: Minutes from the meeting on January 5 2020 approved without modification

Business:

Motion: Owner Sally Honer made a motion to hold baking training seminar on February 26

Vote: 4 for, 1 opposed

Resolved: Motion carried

Motion: Baker Mark Sellers made a motion to host taste testing session during February 26 training seminar

Vote: 5 for, 0 opposed

Resolved: Motion carried

Motion: Associate Abby Morgan made a motion to get rid of worst seller, red velvet cupcakes

Vote: 2 for, 3 opposed

Resolved: Motion failed

Meeting adjourned by Sally Honer, bakery owner, at 3:50 pm.

Case writing

Task: Write minutes for a meeting based on the information below:

A meeting was held by the Research & Development Department of ABC Lively Publishing House at Hilton Hotel at 8:00 am, March 26 2020. Amy Williams(Chair), Kathy Green, Larry Johnson, Bill Trotter, Richard Smith, John Black(secretary) were present, while David Li was absent.

In the meeting:

* the minutes of the meeting held on February 24 2020 was read and approved;

* the past three months' record was presented;

* two proposals were presented at the meeting. Kathy Green suggested a children's fairy tales program. Bill Trotter recommended a set of financing books for housewives. It was unanimously resolved that Bill Trotter's proposal was accepted.

The meeting was adjourned at 11:00 am.

Write in about **120-140** words.

Part F
Further business story

Business Meeting Etiquette

Business meetings are held for a variety of reasons, but one common characteristic is the sharing of information with others. As in dining, there are rules of *etiquette* that goes along with meetings. Unfortunately in our society today, people have got so *technical* and fast-paced that forget about the other person and common *courtesy* at meetings, with the business meeting etiquette lost or ignored.

Business meetings are one *arena* in which poor etiquette can have negative effects. By improving your business meeting etiquette you automatically improve your chances of success. Comfort, trust, *attentiveness* and clear communication are examples of the positive results of demonstrating good etiquette. Proper etiquette can play a fairly significant role in whether a meeting is a productive gathering or an inefficient use of time. Your manners and etiquette are not just actions—they are an attitude—an attitude that is closely related to your self-confidence, your position in business and personal life, as well as your ability to build successful relationships, teams and organizations.

Informal meetings are generally more relaxed affairs and may not necessarily take place in the office or meeting room. Even so, a sense of *professionalism* and good business etiquette are still required. The person calling the meeting (the chair) should be the most *senior* or the one with the most direct or urgent interest in the topic at hand. The chair should decide the time, place and agenda. These details should be confirmed with everyone to make sure all are *in agreement* and no inconvenience is caused. The chair must make the purpose of the meeting clear to the *attendees*, how long it will last and what is expected of them, i.e. particular information or preparation of documents. Failing to *relay* the proper information is bad business etiquette as it could cause embarrassment. *Punctuality* is a must. Keeping people waiting is considered the height of poor etiquette as it *abuses* their time. The chair should *strive to* ensure the meeting stays within a set framework or agenda so that it is kept as short and effective as possible. He/she must *keep* circular disagreements and the like *to a minimum*. The chair should (pre-) appoint someone to record the *proceedings*; documenting major decisions or action points. This can later be distributed to the attendees for reference. If the results of the meeting have an effect on others who were not present, it is considered proper business etiquette to inform them.

The business etiquette of formal meetings such as departmental meetings, management meetings, board meetings, negotiations and the like can be puzzling. Such meetings usually have a set format. For example, the chair may always be the same person, and minutes, agendas or reports may be pre-distributed or voting may take place. Prepare well for the meeting, as your contribution may be *integral* to the proceedings. If you are using statistics, reports or any other information, make sure it has been handed out at least three days prior to the meeting. Dress well and arrive in good time. Your professionalism is linked to both. Always remember to switch off a mobile phone and do not talk on your phone during the meeting. Do not make your presence known by making noises. If there is an established seating pattern, accept it. If you are unsure, ask. Acknowledge any introductions or *opening remarks* with a brief recognition of the chair and other participants. When discussions are under way it is good business etiquette to allow more senior figures to contribute first. Do not carry on a conversation while someone else is talking. Never interrupt anyone—even if you disagree strongly. Note what has been said and return to it later with the chair's permission. When speaking, be brief and ensure what you say is relevant. Always address the chair unless it is clear that others are not doing so. It is a serious *breach* of business etiquette to *divulge* information to others about a meeting. What has been discussed should be considered as confidential.

The underlying principles of the all the above business meeting etiquette *pointers* are good manners, courtesy and consideration. If these principles are *adhered to*, the chances of offense and misunderstandings are greatly reduced.

New words and expressions

arena	*n.*	舞台；竞技场
attendee	*n.*	出席者；在场者
attentiveness	*n.*	注意力；专注
breach	*n.*	违背，违反
circular	*adj.*	（信件、文件等）供传阅的，通知性的
	n.	通知；供传阅的函件、声明
courtesy	*n.*	礼貌；好意
divulge	*vt.*	泄露；暴露
etiquette	*n.*	礼节，礼仪；规矩
integral	*adj.*	重要的；完整的
pointer	*n.*	指针；指示器；指标
proceeding	*n.*	进程；程序；诉讼；事项
professionalism	*n.*	专业性；专家的地位
punctuality	*n.*	严守时间
relay	*vt.*	转播
senior	*adj.*	高级的；年长的；地位较高的；资格较老的
technical	*adj.*	技术上的；专门的
adhere to		坚持
and the like		诸如此类
in agreement		一致；同意；意见一致
keep… to a minimum		保持在最小限度
opening remark		开幕致辞；开场白
strive to		努力

Critical thinking

Work in groups and discuss the following questions.

(1) Why do we need to know business etiquette?

(2) What are the etiquettes of attending a meeting?

(3) How do we practice proper business meeting etiquette?

Unit 6
Customers

In sales, commerce and economics, a customer (sometimes known as a client, buyer, or purchaser) is the recipient of a good, service, product or an idea—obtained from a seller, vendor, or supplier via a financial transaction or exchange for money or some other valuable consideration. An ultimate etymology of "client" may imply someone merely inclined to do business, whereas a purchaser procures goods or services on occasion but a customer customarily or habitually engages in transactions (historically: the collection of tolls or taxes). Such distinctions have no contemporary semantic weight.

Learning objectives

* To understand the meaning of phrases about customers;
* To discuss the importance of customer relations;
* To grasp the gist and spot the details of a listening text about how to entertain clients;
* To familiarize with the tips of writing a sales letter.

Warm-up questions

(1) Where would you find your customers?

(2) What would you do to keep your customers loyal?

Part A
General business vocabulary

1. Match the expressions in the box with the following descriptions.

> A. most valuable customers   B. customer service training
>
> C. brand loyalty   D. customer relationship management (CRM)
>
> E. customer satisfaction   F. loyalty business model
>
> G. customer engagement   H. customer delight
>
> I. service recovery   J. customer experience

(1) It is a measure of how products and services supplied by a company meet or surpass customer expectation.

(2) These customers buy more or higher-value products than the average customer. They are the most profitable for a company, so the companies can provide these customers with advice and guidance to make them loyal.

(3) It can be defined as the internal and personal responses of the customers that might be line with the company either directly or indirectly. In commerce, it is the product of an interaction between an organization and a customer over the duration of their relationship.

(4) It refers to teaching employees the knowledge, skills, and competencies required to increase customer satisfaction.

(5) It is an approach to managing a company's interaction with current and potential future customers that tries to analyze data about customers' history with a company and to improve business relationships with customers, specifically focusing on customer retention and ultimately driving sales growth.

(6) It is a business model used in strategic management in which company resources are employed so as to increase the loyalty of customers and other stakeholders in the expectation that corporate objectives will be met or surpassed.

(7) It is defined as positive feelings towards a brand and dedication to purchase the same product or service repeatedly now and in the future from the same brand, regardless of a competitor's actions or changes in the environment.

(8) It is surprising a customer by exceeding his or her expectations and thus creating a positive emotional reaction. This emotional reaction leads to word of mouth.

(9) It is aiming at converting a previously dissatisfied customer into a loyal customer. It is the action a service provider takes in response to service failure.

(10) It is a business communication connection between an external stakeholder (consumer) and an organization (company or brand) through various channels of correspondence.

2. Listen to the conversations and answer the questions.

(1) Who is loyal to Marks & Spencer?

(2) Which words do Ann and Stephen use to describe the staff at Marks & Spencer?

(3) Which word does Ann use to describe the quality of the products?

(4) How does Stephen do his banking?

(5) How much does the Health Center cost for a year?

(6) What are the opening hours of the center?

(7) What is the procedure for new member?

(8) Is it OK to bring guests? What is the policy for that?

Part B
Reading

What Is a Customer?

[1] What is a customer? Ask this question to anyone in the public or private sector and you are *liable* to receive many *variations* on the same definition in return. You may hear a customer described in terms such as profit units, *components* of a *balanced scorecard*, affecting the bottom line, target markets, market share or key *demographics*. Frequently, customers are only represented as numbers and percentages *captured* in *balance sheets*

and presented in boardrooms on profit and loss statements. A universal truth in business is that organizations primarily think of customers in terms of what they mean to their *bottom line*.

Who is a customer?

[2] Who is the person behind the number? Who is the person that is part of the target market and represents your key demographics? Looking beyond how they are represented in the boardroom, at the most basic, but *elusive*, level of reality, a customer is a human being. More specifically, a customer is a human being with feelings. And everyone has customers, whether they are *internal* and/or *external*, in the form of direct consumers, *constituents*, or business to business. But, when was the last time you attended a meeting and reviewed a financial forecast that *highlighted* how your customers feel they are being treated as individuals? How do they feel about the products and services your organization delivers? How do they feel during *interactions* with your organization?

[3] We acknowledge that yes; all of your customers affect your bottom line. And, the customers' feelings are what help determine the extent to which they will positively or negatively affect your bottom line. You may continue to refer to your customers in terms of *statistics*, market share and key demographics, but never forget that there is a person behind the *terminology*—a person with feelings.

Feelings count

[4] Customers have choices. Rarely are products and services so vastly different or unique that an organization is not threatened by competitive pressures. What causes a customer to choose one product or service over another is the way they feel about the product and how they feel they are treated by the organization. This is particularly evident in the demand today for *stellar service* and its impact on building customer loyalty. Regardless of changes and multiple demands on an organization, one constant drive of *maximizing* sales and *market share* is the daily delivery of stellar service that not only meets customers' expectations, but exceeds them.

[5] Organizations that listen and respond to the way their customers feel will succeed and *thrive* despite changes or demands in the marketplace. *Ultimately*, it's feelings that influence and are responsible for customer loyalty.

New words and expressions

capture	['kæptʃə]	vt.	捕，捕获
component	[kəm'pəʊnənt]	n.	成分；组件
constituent	[kən'stɪtjʊənt]	n.	成分；组成部分

demographics	[ˌdeməˈɡræfɪks]	*n.*	人口统计资料
elusive	[ɪˈluːsɪv]	*adj.*	难懂的；易被忘记的
external	[ɪkˈstɜːnl]	*adj.*	外部的；表面的
highlight	[ˈhaɪlaɪt]	*vt.*	突出；强调
interaction	[ˌɪntərˈækʃn]	*n.*	相互作用
internal	[ɪnˈtɜːnl]	*adj.*	内部的；内在的
liable	[ˈlaɪəbl]	*adj.*	有责任（义务）的；有……倾向的；易……的
maximize	[ˈmæksɪmaɪz]	*vt.*	取……最大值；对……极为重视
statistics	[stəˈtɪstɪks]	*n.*	统计；【统计】统计资料
stellar	[ˈstelə]	*adj.*	恒星的；杰出的
terminology	[ˌtɜːmɪˈnɒlədʒɪ]	*n.*	术语
thrive	[θraɪv]	*vi.*	繁荣，兴旺；茁壮成长
ultimately	[ˈʌltɪmətlɪ]	*adv.*	最后，最终
variation	[ˌveərɪˈeɪʃn]	*n.*	变化；【生物】变异，变种
balance sheet			【会计】资产负债表
balanced scorecard			平衡计分卡；综合评价卡
bottom line			（收益表的）底行；净收益
market share			【贸易】市场占有率
stellar service			星级服务；一流服务

Reading comprehension

1. **Work in pairs and discuss whether the following statements are True (T) or False (F).**

   (1) A customer can be described as profit units, components of a balanced scorecard, affecting the bottom line, target markets, market share or key demographics.

   (2) According to the passage, customers are numbers and percentages captured in balance sheets and presented in boardrooms on profit and loss statements.

   (3) A customer is a human being with feelings.

   (4) The reason why a customer chooses one product or service is not what they feel about the product and how they feel they are treated by the organization.

   (5) Feelings count means that feelings influence and are responsible for customer loyalty.

2. **Choose the best answers to fill in each blank.**

   (1) Once you discover and report this, you're not _____ for money the bank lost, but neither are you entitled to compensation for the time and effort you spend straightening the matter out.

   　　A. required 　　　　**B.** liable 　　　　**C.** complicated 　　　　**D.** relied

(2) As a rule, consumers look for the best values for what they spend while producers seek the best price and _____ for what they have to sell.

    A. service   **B.** money   **C.** profit   **D.** result

(3) The company will give a special _____ of 15% for cash payment.

    A. discount   **B.** offer   **C.** policy   **D.** compensation

(4) The company says that growth of 10% is on _____.

    A. target   **B.** sale   **C.** show   **D.** purpose

(5) Many of the banks offer a poor level of _____ service.

    A. customs   **B.** custom   **C.** customers   **D.** customer

(6) This new market was weighed by some moves in large index _____ Retailing Corporation.

    A. contact   **B.** constituent   **C.** composition   **D.** contract

(7) If they understand how you satisfy your customers, they can understand the link between their performance and _____.

    A. the bottom line   **B.** the top line

    C. the dead line   **D.** the warning line

(8) It's also battled customer losses and a reputation for less-than- _____ service.

    A. poor customer   **B.** stellar customer

    C. loyal customer   **D.** demanding customer

(9) New employees will _____ on them, but they must find out how to meet new challenges themselves.

    A. work   **B.** depend   **C.** focus   **D.** thrive

(10) Besides the gift card, the customers will now have access to the Balance Rewards _____ program.

    A. keeping   **B.** development   **C.** loyalty   **D.** scheme

Part C
Listening

Listen to the four speakers' talks on "How to Entertain Clients". Decide whether the following statements are True (T) or False (F).

(1) We must choose proper types of activities to entertain different clients aiming at making them feel satisfied and comfortable.

(2) We should try to find chances to do business with our clients while entertain them.

(3) Entertaining client shouldn't be done by means of meals or parties.

(4) Well-educated clients may expect some high class-associated activities, but formal meals are still necessary.

(5) The cost of entertainment is not often the essential things.

New words and expressions

budget	['bʌdʒɪt]	*n.*	预算，预算费
criteria	[kraɪ'tɪərɪə]	*n.*	标准，条件（criterion 的复数）
lucrative	['luːkrətɪv]		有利可图的，赚钱的；合算的
negotiate	[nɪ'gəʊʃɪeɪt]	*vt.*	（尤指在商业或政治方面）谈判，协商
orchestra	['ɔːkɪstrə]	*n.*	管弦乐团，管弦乐队
proportional	[prə'pɔːʃənl]	*adj.*	成比例的；相称的
sportswear	['spɔːtsweə]	*n.*	运动装；休闲服
end up			结束，告终
golf course			高尔夫球场
high class			【经】高级，优质
key matter			关键问题
put weight on			强调；着重于

Part D
Translating

Translate the following sentences into English.

(1) 与客户关系的好坏对公司发展有着直接的影响。

(2) 公司在留住老客户的同时，也会想尽一切办法招揽新客户。

(3) 公司的业务是建立在客户忠诚度基础上的。

(4) 从员工那里得到的反馈表明，客户认为我们的质量控制不严格。

(5) 如果客户不满意，他们可能找别人做生意了。

Part E
Writing skills: Sales letter

推销函 (Sales letter)，也叫销售函，是一种主动向潜在客户推销公司产品或服务的信函，具有信息性 (informativeness)、宣传性 (publicity) 和说服性 (persuasion)，即介绍产品或服务的基本信息，宣传企业形象，说服买家采取行动 (购买产品或服务)。

推销函要语言简洁，语气具有鼓动性，并能始终站在买家的立场考虑。推销函是用来向顾客介绍产品或服务的，因此通常采用正式的书信结构，并且无人称，因为信件的接收者不止一个。

推销函常提醒读者考虑一件事——一个必须解决的问题，然后再介绍能够解决这个问题的产品。然后，开始推销产品。大多数读者都知道推销函也就是广告。当然，推销函一般也包含鼓励读者试用产品的优惠，提供的优惠措施必须清楚明白而且能为读者带来有用的服务。

一封好的推销函应该：1) 精心设计吸引人的标题；2) 为客户面对的问题提供解决方案；3) 通过其他客户的评价提高自己的可信度；4) 引导客户采取行动。

一封好的推销函不应该：1) 言过其实，夸大炫耀；2) 低估读者；3) 哗众取宠；4) 讲竞争对手坏话。告诉读者你能做到的，而不是竞争对手无法做到的。

Example

Dear Mr. Harrison,

We at ABC Textiles are glad to inform you about our new product. We are one of the renowned names in the textile industries and have a vast collection of fabrics.

This winter, we have released a new Snow Fabrics line. The products in this line are specially designed to withstand the cold weather and are warmer than our previous designs.

They are also available in dark colors meant to trap the heat in for the best experience. We assure you that your customers will love the Snow Fabrics line.

If you have any queries, please contact ABC Textiles through abctext@website.com or call our office at (123) 456 789 00.

You can also visit our website: www.abctextiles.com.

Sincerely,

Tom Johnson

Marketing Manager,

ABC Textiles

Case writing

Task: Suppose you are working in a training company—CVS. Your company offers a training program on creating and improving teamwork spirit.

Your boss asks you to write to a manager, Mr. Green, to introduce this training program to him.

Write in about **120-140** words.

Part F
Further business story

Keeping Your Customers Loyal

Loyal customers are *at the base* of every successful business whether online or offline. So every business from the very beginning of time has tested and tried many different methods to keep customers loyal to their business and keep them away from their competition. Loyal customers will *undoubtedly* bring you new business *at no cost* to you. The loyal customer will always *brag* to family, friends, and even strangers about where it was that they got such a great deal and fantastic service. No paid advertising in the world can equal what a loyal customer can do for your business. Look over these suggestions and be sure that you are at least using these.

Stay in touch. Stay in contact with customers *on a regular basis*. Ask customers if they want to be updated by e-mail when you make changes to your *website*. Offer them a "Free" *e-zine subscription* after every sale *follow-up* with the customer to see if they are satisfied with their purchase.

Easy communication. Make it easy for your customers to contact you. Offer as many contact methods as possible. Allow customers contact you by e-mail. *Hyperlink* your e-mail address so customers won't have to type it. Offer numbers for phone and fax contacts, and a mailing address.

Friendly website. Make it easy for your customers to *navigate* on your website. Ask them to fill out an electronic survey to find out how to make your website more customer friendly. Have a "*FAQ*" page on your website to explain anything that might *confuse* your customers.

Impress your customer. Give your customers more than they expect. Send thank you gifts to lifetime customers. E-mail them online greeting cards on holidays or birthdays. Award *bonuses* or *discounts* to customers who make a big purchase.

Be nice. Always be polite to your customers. Use the words Please, Thank you, and You're welcome. Be polite to your customers even if they are being *irate* with you. Always apologize to your customers should you make a mistake. Admit your mistakes quickly and make it up to them *in a big way*.

These are just a few *common sense* good business practices and yet you would be amazed at how many websites neglect to follow them. These are simple and yet very effective in establishing *solid* loyal customers that will return to your website time and time again *as opposed to* trying someone new. These business methods have established loyal customers in the *offline* business world for years and work online as well. Review your website to see just how many of these you are using. Then employ those that you are not, and then track the *repeat customers* that you gain.

New words and expressions

bonus	*n.*	奖金；红利；额外津贴
brag	*vi.*	自夸，夸耀，吹嘘（与 about，of 连用）
confuse	*vt.*	使混乱；使困惑
discount	*n.*	折扣；贴现率
e-zine	*abbr.*	电子杂志（Electronic Magazine）
FAQ	*abbr.*	常见问题（Frequently Asked Question）
follow-up	*n.*	跟进，后续行动
hyperlink	*n.*	超链接
irate	*adj.*	生气的，发怒的
navigate	*vt.*	浏览
offline	*adj.*	脱机的；离线的
solid	*adj.*	可靠的
subscription	*n.*	订阅
undoubtedly	*adv.*	确实地，毋庸置疑的
website	*n.*	网页；网址
as opposed to		与……截然相反；对照
at no cost		不花钱；不惜代价
at the base of		在……基础上
common sense		常识
in a big way		大规模地，彻底地
on a regular basis		定期地；经常地
repeat customers		回头客

Critical thinking

Work in groups and discuss the following questions.

(1) What is your understanding about customers?

(2) Why is it important to keep good customer relations?

(3) What are the possible ways to keep customers loyal?

Unit 7
Orders and Payments

In business or commerce, an order is a stated intention, either spoken or written, to engage in a commercial transaction for specific products or services. A payment is the transfer of an item of value from one party (such as a person or company) to another in exchange for the provision of goods, services or both, or to fulfill a legal obligation.

Learning objectives

* To demonstrate an understanding of the vocabulary of orders and payments;
* To list and explain the basic payment options in commercial transactions;
* To evaluate the message about the payment in international trade and make appropriate judgement;
* To compose a persuasive letter.

Warm-up questions

(1) What should be done before a contract is signed?

(2) What are the common methods of payment?

Part A
General business vocabulary

1. Match the words or phrases in the box with the following descriptions.

> A. collection
> C. remittance
> E. Mail Transfer (M/T)
> G. documentary collection
> I. Document against Payment (D/P)
> J. Documents against Acceptance (D/A)
>
> B. Telegraphic Transfer(T/T)
> D. letter of credit
> F. clean collection
> H. Demand Draft (D/D)

(1) It is the transfer of funds, usually from a buyer to a distant seller, instrument of transfer (such as a check or draft), or funds so transferred.

(2) This is a process through which the global banking system acts on behalf of an exporter (or seller) to collect cash payment or a time draft from the importer (or buyer) in return for documents required for taking delivery of the ordered goods.

(3) It is a document, typically from a bank (issuing bank), assuring that a seller (beneficiary) will receive payment up to the amount of the letter of credit, as long as certain documentary delivery conditions have been met.

(4) It refers to a means of transferring funds abroad. The local bank issues a letter of payment by airmail to foreign branches or correspondent bank, for the payment of foreign exchange business.

(5) This is a historic term used to refer to an electronic means of transferring funds abroad.

(6) A bank issues this negotiable instrument to a client (drawer), directing another bank (drawee) or one of its own branches to pay a certain sum to the specified party (payee).

(7) It is the collection whereby only the financial document (draft or bill of exchange) is sent through the banks without a bill of lading and/or other shipping documents (which are sent separately by the consignor to the consignee).

(8) International trade procedure in which a bank in the importer's country acts on behalf of an exporter for collecting and remitting payment for a shipment. The exporter presents the shipping and collection documents to his or her bank (in own country) which sends them to its correspondent bank in the importer's country.

(9) An arrangement in which an exporter instructs a bank to hand over shipping and title documents (see document of title) to an importer only if the importer accepts the accompanying bill of exchange or draft by signing it.

(10) Arrangement under which a buyer can get the delivery (shipping) documents only upon full payment of the invoice or bill of exchange.

2. Listen to the conversations and answer the following questions.

(1) What should the term of payment be for the products mentioned?

(2) Are D/A and D/P acceptable payment terms?

(3) Is installment acceptable?

(4) What documents will the seller provide?

(5) Why should the buyer send L/C one month before the goods are shipped?

(6) Are there any mistakes in the L/C?

(7) Why is the spelling mistake so serious?

(8) Will the seller be held responsible for the delay?

Part B
Reading

Methods of Payments in Global Marketplace

[1] The sale of goods in foreign countries is complicated by the risks encountered when dealing with foreign customers. There are risks from inadequate *credit reports* on customers, problems of *currency exchange controls*, distance, and different legal systems, and the cost and difficulty of collecting *bad debts* that require a different emphasis on payment systems.

[2] When conducting transactions in the domestic market, the typical payment procedure for established customers is an ***open account***. However, the most frequently used term of payment in foreign commercial transactions for both export and import sales is the ***letter of credit***.

[3] The five basic payment options for both importers and exporters in decreasing order of attractiveness for foreign commercial transactions are as follows:

[4] ***Cash in Advance***. The exporter receives payment before the ***shipment*** of goods. This minimizes the exporter's risk and ***financial exposure*** since there is no ***collection risk*** and no interest cost on ***accounts receivable***. However, importers will rarely agree to these terms since it ties up their capital and the goods may not be received.

[5] Letter of Credit. Letters of credit are widely used in international trade since they minimize the risk for both exporter and importer. A letter of credit is a document ***issued*** by the importer's bank guaranteeing to pay the exporter so long as conditions relating to the sale, which are specified in the letter of credit, have been met. An ***irrevocable*** letter of credit, where cancellation or modification of the original terms is not possible without the mutual agreement of both importer and exporter, is usual and best. ***Confirmed letters of credit***, which are supported by not only a foreign bank but also a bank in the exporter's country, are often used. With a confirmed letter of credit, the exporter is guaranteed payment even if the foreign bank does not ***honor*** its commitments.

[6] ***Draft***. This is an order, ***addressed to*** the importer by the exporter, specifying when a given sum of money is due from the importer or its agent. ***Sight drafts*** are payable immediately upon ***presentation*** to the importer or its agent, for example, a bank. ***Time drafts*** are payable at a specified future date. Because of the lag between acceptance and payment, they are a useful financing device.

[7] Open Account. The exporter ships the goods first and bills to the importer later in accordance with the agreed credit terms. Since evidence of the importer's obligation is not as well specified as with other instruments of payment, payment is often difficult to collect if the importer ***defaults***.

[8] ***Consignment***. The exporter ***retains title to*** the goods until the importer has sold them. It is a highly risky method of payment, usually restricted to dealing with ***affiliated companies***. These terms are only offered to very trustworthy importers.

[9] When a company is involved in foreign commercial transactions, it has to choose terms of payment carefully. An experienced exporting firm extends credit cautiously. It evaluates new customers with care and continuously monitors older accounts. Such a firm may wisely decide to decline a customer's request for open account credit if the risk is too great and propose instead payment on delivery terms through a ***documentary sight draft*** or ***irrevocable confirmed letter of credit*** or even payment in advance. On the other hand,

for a fully creditworthy customer, the experienced exporter may decide to allow a month or two to pay, perhaps even on open account.

New words and expressions

consignment	[kən'saɪnmənt]	*n.*	寄售，委托销售
default	[dɪ'fɔːlt]	*vi.*	拖欠，不履行（合同），违约
draft	[drɑːft]	*n.*	汇票
honor	['ɒnə]	*vt.*	遵守
irrevocable	[ɪ'revəkəbl]	*adj.*	不可撤销的
issue	['ɪʃuː]	*vt.*	开具
presentation	[prezn'teɪʃn]	*n.*	展示，出具
shipment	['ʃɪpmənt]	*n.*	装货；装运
account receivable			应收账款
addressed to			对某人开具
affiliated company			附属公司
bad debt			坏账
cash in advance			预付现金
collection risk			托收风险
confirmed letter of credit			保兑信用证
credit report			信用报告
currency exchange control			货币兑换管制
documentary sight draft			跟单即期汇票
financial exposure			财务风险
irrevocable confirmed letter of credit			保兑不可撤销即期信用证
letter of credit			信用证
open account			赊销
retain title to			保留所有权
sight draft			即期汇票
time draft			定期汇票

Reading comprehension

1. **Work in pairs and discuss whether the following statements are True (T) or False (F).**

   (1) Problems of currency exchange controls is one of the difficulties while doing international business.

   (2) The most frequently used term of payment in foreign commercial transactions is the open account.

(3) The exporter receives payment before the shipment of goods for cash in advance.

(4) Draft is an order addressed to the exporter by the importer.

(5) For an open account, it is easy to collect money for the exporter.

2. Choose the best answer to fill in each blank.

(1) This is the most _____ case I have ever handled.
   A. complication   **B.** complicated   **C.** complicate   **D.** compatible

(2) I felt like a fraud, _____ to the task.
   A. inadequate   **B.** irresponsible   **C.** enough   **D.** adequate

(3) The system records all transactions _____ the firm and its suppliers.
   A. on   **B.** in   **C.** between   **D.** of

(4) It is the correct procedure _____ hiring new staff.
   A. for   **B.** with   **C.** on   **D.** under

(5) They banned smoking to _____ the danger of fire.
   A. lift   **B.** less   **C.** lighten   **D.** minimize

(6) Too much _____ to strong sunlight can cause skin burns.
   A. contact   **B.** exposure   **C.** touch   **D.** exhibition

(7) There was no obvious _____ of a break-in.
   A. evidence   **B.** reason   **C.** suspect   **D.** witness

(8) Doctors are _____ by law to keep patients alive while there is a chance of recovery.
   A. ruled   **B.** obliged   **C.** restricted   **D.** demanded

(9) He _____ in his payments on the loan.
   A. failed   **B.** didn't conduct   **C.** faulted   **D.** defaulted

(10) They affiliated themselves _____ the same political party.
   A. at   **B.** on   **C.** with   **D.** of

Part C
Listening

Listen to the conversation "Urging the Buyer to Open the L/C". Decide whether the following statements are True (T) or False (F).

(1) The sellers cannot start shipment because they haven't received the L/C yet.

(2) The sellers call the buyers because there are some mistakes in the L/C.

(3) The steamer "Santa Maria" is due from Shanghai in the middle of October.

(4) The sellers will call their bank to open the L/C immediately.

(5) Mr. Foster is from the buyers' company.

New words and expressions

due	[djuː]	*adj.*	到期的；即将启航
inquire	[ɪnˈkwaɪə]	*vi.*	询问；查究；询价
relevant	[ˈreləvənt]	*adj.*	相关的
steamer	[ˈstiːmə]	*n.*	轮船；蒸汽机；蒸笼
urgent	[ˈɜːdʒənt]	*adj.*	紧急的；急迫的
a long distance call			长途电话
CNIEC (China National Import and Export Corporation)			中国进出口公司
delivery date			交货日期
on top of the world			幸福到极点
open the L/C			开立信用证
ready for shipment			准备装船
there's a good chance			可能性很大

Part D
Translating

Translate the following sentences into English.

(1) 我们将按托收方式向你方开出即期跟单汇票。

(2) 我们不同意开具 30 天期的承兑交单汇票。

(3) 订货货款以 60 天信用证或即期付款交单方式支付。

(4) 百分之五十用信用证，其余的用付款交单，您看怎么样？

(5) 欧洲的许多银行能够开立信用证，而且用人民币支付。

Part E
Writing skills: Persuasive letter

写作提示

当你和银行、保险公司、政府机构、雇主打交道的时候，可能会遇到麻烦。这时，你需要写一封劝导信（Persuasive letter），来劝说别人去做某件事，或者帮助你。劝导信是一种正式的沟通方式，但通常采用的是半正式的语气。在直邮营销或对一种新产品阐述看法的时候也可以采用劝导信。

劝导信有独特的格式。劝导信应当能够吸引读者的注意力，实际上，劝导信的写作是一门艺术。整封信都要采取谈话的语气。写作者要预测读者会有什么疑问，并做出解答。这需要写作者了解读者的心理。劝导信必须打印在具有公司信头的公司信纸上，要避免在信中顾左右而言他，应当直奔主题。信的开头部分要吸引人，尽快提出提议，只有这样才能抓住读者的眼球。如果提议不够好，那么劝导信就毫无用处。所以要让你的建议无法抵抗，使读者想要立刻拿起电话，了解更多内容。劝导信的句子应当简洁，段落应当简短。

Example

Really Amazing Resorts
Miami, FL
Contact: 0123-1144-5623
E-mail: ra@hotels.com

Date: November 1, 2012

To

Mr. Jerry Stone,

Annabelle Corp.

Orlando, FL

Dear Mr. Stone,

　　Here is an Offer too Good to Refuse! Before you roll your eyes thinking, "Oh God! Not another one!", and chuck this letter into a bin. Just read a few of the lines below.

　　Imagine the mellow sun and the grainy sand. Imagine the soft rolling of the waves of the sea, those beautiful sunsets in the evening. Watch all of this in the lap of luxury, sipping your choicest drink. Imagine a week's getaway from all the traffic noise that wakes you up, that crazy drive to work, the yelling and screaming at workplace and at home. Imagine a place where you can sleep when you want, wake up when you want, do what you want, and live the way YOU like!

Sounds great, doesn't it?

Welcome to Really Amazing Resorts. At RA resorts, we promise to deliver the best of the service, the best food, the BEST of everything just for you.

One of our patrons recently said, "I come here harrowed and troubled. But I go back a different man. The place and its natural beauty really change me. I sure will be making the short trip from New Jersey to here next time. My wife says I'm becoming too grumpy!"

On account of our first anniversary, we're giving you a flat 65% discount on rooms and 40% discount on menu price of foods and beverages! So hurry. Call 0123-1144-5623 to know more.

Thank you!

Sincerely,

Barry Cromwell

Guest Relations Manager

Really Amazing Resorts

Case writing

Task: ABC Cruise Vacations is offering week-long holidays on their cruise ships at a 50% discount over their normal rates. Write a persuasive letter to persuade a potential customer to get on board.

Write in about **120-140** words.

Part F

Further business story

How to Write Sales Contracts

The definition and forms of a sales contract

In international trade a sales contract is a legal document made by and entered into between a seller and a buyer on the basis of their negotiation. In the contract the right and obligation of both parties are definitely **stipulated**. The contract is binding on them both.

When, in the course of business negotiation, an *offer* with *engagement* or a *counter-offer* of this kind is accepted, the transaction is completed and a contractual relationship between the *offeror* and the *offeree* is concluded. However, in keeping with regular practice in international trade, a written contract or *confirmation* is usually signed to *bind* both the seller and the buyer.

The content of a sales contract

Generally speaking, sales contract includes three parts, *the opening part*, the body of the contract, and *the closing part*. The opening part usually includes the name of the contract, contract number, contract award date, relevant parties' (the buyer and the seller) name and address, and the willingness to sign the contract and the guarantee to carry out the contract. The closing part is usually the signature of the relevant parties. The body of a sales contract consists of:

1) Commodity name and *specification*

Examples:

S235 Christmas bears with caps and scarves, as per the samples dispatched by the seller on August 20. 2012

Sesame seeds, Moisture (max.) 8%, *Admixture* (max.) 6%, Oil content (min.) 48%

Chinese grey duck's *down* with 18% down content, 1% more or less allowed

2) Quantity

Examples:

Chinese rice 10,000 metric tons, 5% more or less at seller's option

Chinese peanut, *gross for net*, 5% more or less at seller's option at contract price

3) Packing

Terms of packing include the material of packing, packing method, the cost of packing, and *marks*.

Examples:

××× to be packed in wooden cases containing 30 pcs of 40 yds each

To be packed in poly bags, 25 pounds in a bag, 4 bags in a sealed wooden case which *is lined with* metal. The cost of packing is for seller's account.

4) Price

Examples:

USD 3.5 per piece *FOB* Shanghai

USD 40 per metric ton cifc 5 New York (or CIF New York including 5% commission)

5) Shipment

Terms of shipment include time of shipment, *port of shipment* and *port of destination, transshipment* and *partial shipment.*

Example:

Shipment not later than July 31, 2017

Port of shipment: Shanghai

Port of destination: London

During June/July in two shipments, transshipment is *prohibited*

6) Insurance

Terms of shipment include who is to insure the goods, risks to be covered, the amount insured, and so on.

Example:

Insurance to be covered by the sellers for 110% of the *invoice value* against all risks and war risks *as per* or subject to *Ocean Marine Cargo Clause* of the People's Insurance Company of China dated January 1, 1981.

7) Payment

Terms of payment include method of payment and time of payment. Examples:

Upon first presentation the buyer shall pay against *documentary draft* drawn by the sellers at sight. The *shipping documents* are to be delivered against payment only.

The buyer shall open through a bank acceptable to the seller an *Irrevocable Letter of Credit payable at sight* to reach the seller 30 days before the month of shipment, *valid for negotiation* in China until the 15th day after the date of shipment.

S/C No. : <u>9903 HW</u>

Examples: Date: <u>2016.04.12</u>

The Seller: Adamas Trading Company Limited	The Buyer: H. Woods & Co.Ltd
Address: No. 121 Guangdong Road,	Address: Nesson House, 37 Newwell
Shanghai, China	Street, London, UK
Fax: 02161433759	FAX: 0176231616

We hereby confirm having sold to you the following goods on terms and conditions as stated below:

Commodity & Specifications	Quantity	Unit Price (US$)	Amount(US$)
"Fairy" Brand Dressing Bag		CIF Liverpool	
1740/A2	1,800/DOZ	USD 12.25/DOZ	USD 22,050
1740/G-006	1,800/DOZ	USD 13.23/DOZ	USD 23,814
As samples ST#22 ST#36 Provided by the sellers on March 30			
Total	3,600/DOZ		USD 45,864

Total contract value: Pay us dollars fourty-five thousand eight hundred and sixty-four only

Packing: In cartons of 10 dozen each, each bag has a tag with "washable" printed

Shipment; To liverpool, May/June/July equal monthly with transshipment not allowed

Terms of payment: By sight negotiation L/C to reach the sellers before April 5

Insurance: For 110% of invoice value against all risks and war risks

Confirmed by

The Seller (signature)		The Buyer (signature)

New words and expressions

admixture	*n.*	混合；添加物；掺和剂
bind	*vt.*	约束
CIF	*abbr.*	到岸价（Cost Insurance and Freight）
confirmation	*n.*	确认；确认书
counter-offer	*n.*	还价；还盘
down	*n.*	羽绒，绒毛
engagement	*n.*	契约，承诺
FOB	*abbr.*	离岸价格；船上交货价格（Free on Board）
mark	*n.*	唛头
offer	*n.*	报价，报盘
offeree	*n.*	受盘人；被发价人
offeror	*n.*	报价人；发盘人
prohibit	*vt.*	禁止
specification	*n.*	规格；详述
stipulate	*vt.*	规定
transshipment	*n.*	转船
as per		按照，依据
be lined with		镶有
documentary draft		跟单汇票
gross for net		以毛作净，以毛重作净重
invoice value		发票金额
Irrevocable Letter of Credit payable at sight		即期不可撤销的信用证
Ocean Marine Cargo Clause		《海洋运输货物保险条款》
partial shipment		分批装运
port of destination		目的港
port of shipment		装货港；装运港
shipping document		货运单据，装运单据

terms of payment	支付条款
the closing part	结尾部分
the opening part	开头部分
valid for negotiation	议付有效

Critical thinking

Work in groups and discuss the following questions.

(1) What is the most common method of payment in international trade? Why?

(2) Which method of payment is the most favorable to the seller? Which is the most favorable to the buyer?

(3) What information should be included in a sales contract?

Unit 8
Advertising

Advertising is a form of marketing communication used to promote or sell something, usually a business's product or service. Commercial ads seek to generate increased consumption of their products or services through "branding", which associates a product name or image with certain qualities in the minds of consumers.

Learning objectives

* To understand the marketing methods;
* To list and explain the types of advertising;
* To identify the tactics of campaign in the listening text;
* To design a questionnaire.

Warm-up questions

(1) How many advertising media channels do you know? What are their advantages and disadvantages?

(2) What are the purposes of advertising?

Part A
General business vocabulary

1. **Match the words or phrases in the box with the following descriptions.**

A. media	B. commercial advertising	C. end-user
D. deceptive advertising	E. target market	F. slogan
G. soft sell	H. market segmentation	I. advertiser
J. advertising agency		

(1) It is a kind of advertising that involves commercial interests rather than advocating a social or political cause.

(2) It is a presentation, omission, act or practice that is likely to mislead consumers.

(3) This term means the person who actually uses a product, whether or not they are the one who purchases the product.

(4) It refers to a group of vehicles used to convey information, news, entertainment and advertising messages to an audience. These include televisions, cable televisions, magazines, radios, billboards, etc.

(5) This is a group of individuals who collectively, are intended recipients of an advertiser's message.

(6) It is the manufacturer, service company, retailer, or supplier who advertises their product or service.

(7) It is a service-based business dedicated to creating, planning, and handling advertising (and sometimes other forms of promotion) for its clients.

(8) This is a brief attention-getting phrase used in advertising or promotions.

(9) It means to divide a market by a strategy directed at gaining a major portion of sales to a subgroup in a category, rather than a more limited share of purchases by all category users.

(10) This is the technique of using low pressure appeals in advertisements and commercials.

2.   Listen to the conversations and answer the questions.

(1) What does the advertiser choose as the advertising media?

(2) Do they do their own printing?

(3) What product do they want an advertisement for?

(4) What does the chairman think of as a good advertising medium?

(5) What is the effect of the magazine ad?

(6) Will the idea of a free advertisement work?

(7) What media did they choose for the T-shirts?

(8) What are the functions of advertisement?

Part B
Reading

Types of Advertising

[1] Different advertisers try to reach different types of audiences. Advertising has taken on many different forms. Commercial advertising media can include wall paintings, billboards, street furniture components, printed *flyers,* radio, cinema and television ads, *web banners,* shopping carts, posters, and the backs of event tickets and supermarket receipts. Any place an "identified" sponsor pays to deliver their message through a medium is advertising. So if we categorize advertisements by the media they use, there will be newspaper advertising, magazine advertising, television advertising, billboard advertising, package advertising, radio advertising, poster advertising, *POP advertising*, *direct mail advertising*, etc.

[2] We'll examine some major types of advertising according to their media. The first one is newspaper advertising. Newspaper advertising has been around longer than any other form of advertising we see today and is still the first kind of advertising that businesses think about doing. It is a good way to reach a large number of people, especially those aged 45-plus who tend to read the paper more frequently than younger *demographic*

groups who tend to get their news from television, radio or the Internet. Most newspapers make nearly all their money from advertising. For that reason, newspapers are inexpensive to buy, and some are free. The portion of the newspaper that is not advertising is called editorial content. In recent years, the *advertorial* emerged. Advertorials are most commonly recognized as an opposite-editorial, which third-parties pay a fee to have included in the paper. Advertorials commonly advertise new products or techniques, such as a new design for golf equipment, a new form of laser surgery, or weight-loss drugs. The tone is usually closer to that of a press release than of an objective news story. The advertising content of a newspaper can be divided into two parts, classified and display. *Classified ads* are small, text-only item obtained via telephone and set into the format by the classified advertising representative. *Display ads* are obtained by sales representatives employed by the newspaper who actively *solicit* local businesses for this larger, more visually oriented ad space.

[3] Television advertisement is a form of advertising in which goods, services, organizations, ideas, etc. are promoted via the medium of television. Most commercials are produced by an outside advertising agency and *airtime* is purchased from a Media Agency or direct from the TV channel or network. The first television advertisement was broadcast in the United States at 14:29 on July 1, 1941. For catching attention of consumers, communication agencies make wide use of humor. Many television advertisements feature *catchy jingles* or *catch-phrases* that generate *sustained appeal*, which may remain in the minds of television viewers long after the *span* of the advertising campaign.

[4] Advertisements of this sort have been used to sell every product imaginable over the years, from household products to goods and services, to political campaigns. *Animation* is often used in advertisements. Techniques can vary from hand-drawn traditional animation to different forms of computer animation. By using animated characters, an advertisement may have a certain appeal that is difficult to achieve with actors or mere product displays.

[5] Increasingly, other media are overtaking television due to a shift towards consumer's usage of the Internet as well as devices such as *TiVo*. Prices of web-based advertising space are dependent on the "relevance" of the surrounding web content and the *traffic* that the website receives. E-mail advertising is another channel. *Unsolicited bulk* e-mail advertising is known as "*spam*". Some companies have proposed to place messages or corporate *logos* on the side of booster rockets and the International Space Station. Controversy exists on the effectiveness of *subliminal advertising*, and the pervasiveness of mass messages.

[6] Other advertising media include SMS (Short Message Service) text messages, word of

mouth advertising, etc. Advertisers must choose the right media to target different consumers.

New words and expressions

advertorial	[ˌædvɜː'tɔːrɪəl]	*n.*	社论式广告
airtime	['eətaɪm]	*n.*	开播时间;(尤指电台或电视台)商业广告的开播时间
animation	[ænɪ'meɪʃn]	*n.*	动画
appeal	[ə'piːl]	*n.*	吸引力,感染力
bulk	[bʌlk]	*adj.*	大批的,大量的
catchy	['kætʃɪ]	*adj.*	引人注意的;容易记住的
demographic	[ˌdemə'græfɪk]	*adj.*	人口统计学的;人口学的
flyer	['flaɪə]	*n.*	传单
jingle	['dʒɪŋgl]	*n.*	歌谣
logo	['ləʊgəʊ]	*n.*	徽标
solicit	[sə'lɪsɪt]	*v.*	征求;招揽
spam	[spæm]	*n.*	垃圾邮件
span	[spæn]	*n.*	跨度,持续时间,时间段
sustained	[sə'steɪnd]	*adj.*	持续的;持久的;持久不变的
TiVo		*abbr.*	硬盘数字录像机
traffic	['træfɪk]	*n.*	浏览量
unsolicited	[ʌnsə'lɪsɪtɪd]	*adj.*	未经请求的;主动提供的
catch-phrase			宣传标语,口号
classified ad			分类广告
direct mail advertising			直邮广告
display ad			展示广告
POP advertising			(point-of-purchase advertising)购物点广告
subliminal advertising			潜意识广告;隐性广告
web banner			网页横幅广告

Reading comprehension

1. Work in pairs and discuss the following questions according to the passage.

   (1) What do commercial advertising media include?

   (2) Who might be influenced by newspaper advertising?

   (3) What are the two main types of newspaper advertisements?

   (4) Why do communication agencies use humor a lot?

   (5) What is a spam?

2. **Choose the best answer to fill in each blank.**

(1) There is a very, very changing _____ situation in the American South and its political culture has to respond to that.
   A. geographic   **B.** photographic   **C.** demographic   **D.** autographic

(2) They were _____ signatures in every street for the sports.
   A. soliciting   **B.** unsolicited   **C.** solitude   **D.** recruiting

(3) You need to think of an informative and _____ title.
   A. scratchy   **B.** catchy   **C.** screechy   **D.** catching

(4) He started his career by writing advertising _____.
   A. jangles   **B.** jungles   **C.** pranks   **D.** jingles

(5) Without correct leadership, the enthusiasm of the masses cannot be _____.
   A. obtained   **B.** contained   **C.** sustained   **D.** stained

(6) People lived shorter lives and so they didn't get far enough into the age _____ to suffer from the chronic diseases that people are suffering more today.
   A. pan   **B.** span   **C.** space   **D.** spam

(7) The show combines _____, music, large puppets and human actors to create a series of funny and creative lessons.
   A. animal   **B.** amanita   **C.** anatomy   **D.** animation

(8) I had a lot of _____ advice from electrical engineers.
   A. unsolicited   **B.** solicited   **C.** solicit   **D.** soliciting

(9) Big purchasers get better pricing because when you buy in _____ you can negotiate a better price.
   A. bull   **B.** bulky   **C.** bunk   **D.** bulk

(10) In exchange, she let them put their company _____ on the video.
   A. log   **B.** luggage   **C.** logo   **D.** legend

Part C
Listening

Listen to the business story "Destin Chamber of Commerce". Decide whether the following statements are True (T) or False (F).

(1) Around two to three thousand tourists arrive from the upper US and Canada to Destin each year.

(2) Most tourists to Destin come from the states north of and surrounding Florida.

(3) Destin was recently ranked by *USA Today* as the best resort in America.

(4) The tourist season of Destin is winter.

(5) They believe the website is the best media for this campaign.

New words and expressions

account	[ə'kaʊnt]	*n.*	委托的广告业务，顾客给予广告商的广告业务
anyhow	['enɪhaʊ]	*adv.*	总之；无论如何；不管怎样
captivating	['kæptɪveɪtɪŋ]	*adj.*	迷人的；有魅力的
constraint	[kən'streɪnt]	*n.*	约束
coupon	['kuːpɒn]	*n.*	赠券
info	['ɪnfəʊ]	*n.*	信息；情报
metropolitan	[metrə'pɒlɪtn]	*adj.*	大都市的
outdoor	['aʊtdɔː]	*adj.*	户外的
PR		*abbr.*	公共关系（public relations）
promo	['prəʊməʊ]	*n.*	商品广告；商品推销
resort	[rɪ'zɔːt]	*n.*	凭借，手段；度假胜地
tactics	['tæktɪks]	*n.*	策略；战术
brainstorming session			集体讨论会
break for lunch			午休；吃午饭
bumper-to-bumper traffic			拥堵的交通
go big			做大，大举行动
in a row			连续
run the numbers			量化的分析
weed out			除去杂草，淘汰，除去

Part D
Translating

Translate the following sentences into English.

(1) 广告文案写作是通过书面和口头文字描述的方式，表达某个品牌所具有的价值和益处的过程。

(2) 许多广告依靠如优惠券、竞赛、回扣等促销方式来刺激人们购买。

(3) 比起一般的印刷广告，读者能够更直接地看到网络广告。有时，当读者从一个网页浏览到另一个网页时，网上广告会自动弹出。

(4) 电视的声音效果和视觉刺激能分散观众对平面广告文字的注意力。

(5) 在杂志上做广告有很多优势，包括能接触目标受众、接纳性高、生命周期长、视觉效果好，以及推广促销的手段好。

Part E
Writing skills: Questionnaire

写作提示

调查问卷 (Questionnaire) 又称调查表或询问表，是以问题的形式系统地记录调查内容的一种问卷。问卷可以是表格式、卡片式或簿记式。设计问卷是询问调查的关键。完美的问卷必须具备两个功能，即能将问题传达给被问的人，以及使被问者乐于回答。要完成这两个功能，问卷设计时应当遵循一定的原则和程序，运用一定的技巧。

问卷表的一般结构有标题、说明、主体、编码号、致谢语和实验记录六项。从形式上看，问题可分为开放式和封闭式两种；从内容上看，可以分为事实性问题、意见性问题、断定性问题、假设性问题和敏感性问题等。

Example

A Questionnaire on Detergent Products

Thank you for answering the following questions. After you finish it, please return this paper in the enclosed self-addressed stamped envelope before June 28, 2020.

1. Which brand or brands of detergent do you often use? (Please tick one brand or more.)

Tide □   Ariel □   Nice □   OMO □   White Cat □
Others □ _____

2. Why do you choose it/them? (Please tick one or more.)
Easy to get.   □
Your friends introduce it/ them to you.   □

The advertising on TV influences your decision. ☐

You have tried it/them before you buy it/ them. ☐

Other reasons: ☐

_____

3. Over the past year, how often have you ordered the brand(s)? (Please tick one.)

Seldom.	☐	10-20 times.	☐
1-10 time(s).	☐	20 or more times.	☐

4. Overall how do you rate your satisfaction with the brand(s)?

Very satisfied.	☐	Somewhat dissatisfied.	☐
Somewhat satisfied.	☐	Very dissatisfied.	☐

Optional:

Name: _____

Address: _____

Occupation: _____

Thank you for taking the time to answer these questions.

Case writing

Task: New Concept Bookstore wants to find out their customers' preferences. Design a questionnaire including the following information:

• the books the readers want to find;

• the frequency of their visits to the bookstore;

• the rate of satisfaction with the quality of the books;

• the rate of convenience of getting the books they want;

• their comments and suggestions.

Write in about **120-140** words.

Part F
Further business story

History of Coca-Cola Company and Its Advertising

Asa Candler's most urgent task was to introduce the new product to the American people. Therefore, he gave away coupons for *complimentary* first tastes of Coca-Cola, and as Coke still was distributed with *pharmacists'* mainly, he *outfitted* distributing pharmacists with clocks, *urns,* calendars and *apothecary scales* bearing the Coca-Cola brand. This *aggressive* promotion worked, and soon *syrup* plants were built up in Chicago, Dallas and Los Angeles. In 1894 the drink was put into bottles for the first time, but it wasn't until 1899 that this was done in a great style. It is worth mentioning here that in 1895 Coca-Cola hired the first *celebrity*, music hall performer Hilda Clark, to promote their product in advertisements.

In 1911 the annual advertising budget of Coca-Cola reached $1 million. No wonder other companies wanted to share in their profits. Around 1912 the first *copycat* beverages appeared, for example King-Cola, which used the same type of writing and colors as Coca-Cola. In reaction to the imitations, Coca-Cola focused on its *authenticity*, with slogans like "Demand the *genuine*" or "Accept no *substitute*", and by creating the new "*Contour* Bottle", i.e. the Coke bottle as we know it today, tried to distinguish itself. In 1916, first president Candler *resigned* and sold the company two years later.

From 1923 the company was led by Roberts Woodruff for nearly 60 years. He wanted to establish Coke in as many different countries as possible. So in 1928 Coca-Cola was visible with the US team during the Amsterdam Olympics; the logo could be found on the walls of bullfighting *arenas* in Spain and on racing dog *sleds* in Canada. Furthermore, to make it easier for people to drink Cola, Coca-Cola developed the *six-pack*, the *open top cooler* and a *vending machine*. In 1931, the world famous image of Santa first appeared on ads.

During World War Ⅱ, Coca-Cola tried to accompany the American soldiers where they went and give them a "taste of home". As a consequence, Cola was enjoyed by lots of non-American people during the war, using ads to give them the feeling they would be supported by Coca-Cola. After the war, Coca-Cola promoted its image as part of a fun, *carefree* American lifestyle, showing happy couples at a *drive-in* or carefree moms driving big yellow *convertibles* on their ads, thus reflecting the spirit of the 50s.

After 75 years of success, Coca-Cola decided to expand with new flavors: in 1961 "Sprite" was put on the market, in 1963 "TAB" and three years later "Fresca". To ease access to Cola for its customers, Coca-Cola introduced the first *lift-top cans* in 1964. The dynamic "Coke Waves" were introduced in 1970. During the 1970s, Coke promoted itself as totally *in tune with* the fun, playfulness and freedom many people were searching for at the time. A big success was the commercial of 1971 showing an international group of young people on a hilltop in Italy, singing "I'd Like to Buy the World a Coke". Remember, this was the time of the peace movement, too.

In 1981 the company got a new chairman—Roberto C. Goizueta. He was responsible for marketing Diet Coke, which was very successful in a society increasingly watching their weight and health. In 1985 Coca-Cola promoted an image of helping to the environment by introducing *recyclable* plastic cans. The same year Cola became the first soft drink ever in space. Also in 1985, the introduction of a new taste of Coca-Cola and the reintroduction of Coca-Cola classic and the original formula led to multiple slogans. 1985 featured "America's Real Choice", while by 1986, two slogans were used to differentiate the brands, with "Red, White & You" for Coca-Cola classic and "Catch the Wave" for Coca-Cola. In 1986, the 100th birthday of the company was celebrated with a lot of publicity and a special Coca-Cola edition.

In the 1990s, Coca-Cola stressed its image as a sport-loving and supporting company. Not only did it sponsor the Olympic Games in Atlanta, 1996, but also the FIFA World Cup football, the Rugby World Cup and the National Basketball Association. In 1993, the still famous slogan "Always Coca-Cola" and the cute polar bear were introduced into the ads.

In January 2003, another slogan for Coca-Cola was introduced—"Coca-Cola... Real". The campaign reflects genuine, *authentic* moments in life and the natural role Coca-Cola plays in them.

In 2006, Coca-Cola introduced My Coke Rewards, a customer loyalty campaign where consumers earn *virtual* "points" by entering codes from special marked packages of Coca-Cola products into a website. There points can in turn be *redeemed* for various prizes or *sweepstakes entries*.

New words and expressions

aggressive	*adj.*	侵略性的；好斗的；有进取心的
arena	*n.*	舞台；竞技场
authentic	*adj.*	真正的，真实的；可信的
authenticity	*n.*	真货地位，正宗性
carefree	*adj.*	无忧无虑的；不负责的
celebrity	*n.*	名人
complimentary	*adj.*	赠送的，免费的
contour	*n.*	轮廓，外形
convertible	*n.*	敞篷车

copycat	adj.	山寨的，模仿的
drive-in	n.	免下车餐馆；免下车电影院
genuine	adj.	真实的，真正的
outfit	v.	配备；供应
pharmacist	n.	药剂师
recyclable	adj.	可回收利用的，可再循环的
redeem	v.	兑换
resign	vt.	辞职；放弃
six-pack	n.	六罐装
sled	n.	雪橇
substitute	n.	替代品；代替者
syrup	n.	糖浆，果汁；含药糖浆
urn	n.	咖啡壶
virtual	adj.	虚拟的
apothecary scale		药剂天平
in tune with		（与……）一致；（与……）协调
lift-top can		易拉罐
open top cooler		上开型冷却器，上开型冷藏柜
sweepstakes entry		抽奖
vending machine		自动售货机

Critical thinking

Work in groups and discuss the following questions.

(1) What makes an effective advertisement?

(2) What is the new trend in advertisement now?

(3) What should advertisers consider when they choose the forms of advertisement for their products or services?

Unit 9
Business Travel

A business trip is a trip undertaken for work or business purposes, as opposed to other types of travel, such as for leisure purposes or regularly commuting between one's home and workplace. The necessity to conduct business travel may have many reasons. A few are stated below:

- visiting customers or suppliers;
- meetings at other company locations;
- marketing or promoting a new or an existing product.

Learning objectives

* To discuss business travels with appropriate words;
* To understand business travels;
* To listen and grasp the tips booking a flight seat;
* To describe graphs.

Warm-up questions

(1) How often do you travel? Where do you like to go?

(2) What kind of hotel do you like to stay in when you are on holiday or on business?

Part A
General business vocabulary

1. **Match the words or phrases in the box with the following descriptions.**

A. round trip	B. boarding pass
C. cancellation	D. itinerary
E. first class (of airplanes)	F. economy class (of airplanes)
G. jet lag	H. flight attendant
I. business class(of airplanes)	J. reimbursement

(1) This physiological condition results from alterations to the body's circadian rhythms because of rapid long-distance transmeridian (east—west or west—east) travel on high-speed aircraft.

(2) It is the act of cancelling or not operating a scheduled flight.

(3) This document is provided by an airline during check-in, giving a passenger permission to board the airplane for a particular flight.

(4) A trip from one destination to another and then returning to the starting location.

(5) This refers to a member of the crew (staff) of an airplane who is responsible for the comfort and safety of its passengers.

(6) The money that the company returns to someone for legitimate and documented expenses that are incurred while traveling on business.

(7) It refers to the most luxurious and expensive class of an airplane.

(8) This class on an airplane generally has the largest number of seats at the lowest prices.

(9) In the airline industry, it was originally intended as an intermediate level of service between economy class and first class, but many airlines now offer this class as the highest level of service, having eliminated first class seating.

(10) This itemized schedule of travel events usually shows an employee's arrival and departure times across various destinations, hotel stay, meetings and appointments.

2. Listen and discuss what are the conversations about? Choose from below.

(1) Making a room reservation (on the phone)

(2) Going through customs

(3) Asking for services

(4) Checking in at a hotel

(5) Checking in at the airport

(6) Booking air tickets

(7) Checking out at a hotel

Part B
Reading

A Glimpse into a Business Travel

[1] Business travel often involves traveling away from one's home for more than one day, in relation to business, professional, or job-related responsibilities. Like many business people, I need to **undertake** international travel from time to time for my import-export company. I encountered many different situations during these trips. Some are interesting, while others may be a little troublesome.

[2] Last May, I visited the United States for one week to meet with some **business contacts**. The flight from Hong Kong to Chicago was smooth although long, and I landed early in the morning Chicago time, which by then was nighttime in Asia. I went to the passport control area and **queued up** at the visitors' **entry counter**. There were about 30 to 40 visitors in front of me so I needed to wait patiently for my turn. I saw that we were organized one behind another with two officers directing us to the proper counter. Everything moved along and it was not **chaotic** at all. A female Asian-American police officer was among the **security personnel assigned** to the area. A sign warned us not to turn on our mobile phones and that anyone who broke that rule could have their phones **confiscated**! Since I was no longer **aboard** the aircraft, I was a bit puzzled about this

restriction and couldn't imagine why using a cell-phone would be a problem. I have since learned this is another security *precaution*.

[3] It took about 15 minutes for me to reach the front of the line and be directed to an *immigration* officer who asked me a few questions. Being satisfied with my responses, she asked me to put my right and left *index fingers* on a screen, one at a time, for electronic *fingerprint scanning*. I followed the instructions: she put a *stamp* on my *Passport* and *granted my entry* in to the United States. The whole process took only two to three minutes and I did not experience any problems.

[4] Although when traveling to other countries it has not been necessary for me to go through fingerprint scanning, my personal feeling is that the extra measures now required by the United States cause me only a little extra inconvenience. I don't believe that the personal data the US authorities *obtained* from me will *pose* any risk of harm to me personally or to my country and, by requiring it of all visitors, it helps them to ensure the safety of their homeland.

[5] I remember that we also suffered *drawbacks* after the 9/11 terrorist attacks. I feel that it is in our interests as well to see that the United States remains a safe and prosperous country for its citizens. The cost that I , a visitor, now pay for doing my part for better security is *minimal*, and one which I am quite happy to bear.

New words and expressions

aboard	[ə'bɔːd]	*adv.*	在飞机上；在船上；在火车上
assign	[ə'saɪn]	*vt.*	分配；指派
chaotic	[keɪ'ɒtɪk]	*adj.*	混乱的
confiscate	['kɒnfɪskeɪt]	*vt.*	没收；充公
drawback	['drɔːbæk]	*n.*	缺点；不利条件
immigration	[ɪmɪ'greɪʃn]	*n.*	外来移民；移居
minimal	['mɪnɪml]	*adj.*	最低的；最小限度的
obtain	[əb'teɪn]	*vi.vt.*	获得
passport	['pɑːspɔːt]	*n.*	护照
pose	[pəʊz]	*vt.*	造成；形成
precaution	[prɪ'kɔːʃn]	*n.*	预防；警惕；预防措施
stamp	[stæmp]	*vt.*	标出；盖章
undertake	[ʌndə'teɪk]	*vt.*	承担；从事
business contact			业务往来；有业务往来的人员或公司
entry counter			入境检台
fingerprint scanning			指纹扫描
granted one's entry			准许进入；准许入境

index finger	食指
queue up	排队
security personnel	安检人员

Reading comprehension

1. **Work in pairs and discuss the following questions according to the passage.**

    (1) Why did the author visit the United States?

    (2) Was the airport in chaos while they were waiting at the passport control area after landing?

    (3) What would happen if people turned on their mobile phones while waiting?

    (4) Which fingers did the author put on the screen for fingerprint scanning?

    (5) Did the author feel offended by the strict security measures?

2. **Choose the best answer to fill in each blank.**

    (1) I want you to _____ all the responsibility.
       A. tackle   **B.** guarantee   **C.** contract   **D.** undertake

    (2) Things have been getting _____ in the stock market recently.
       A. chaotic   **B.** confusion   **C.** chaos   **D.** noisy

    (3) The teacher _____ my cell-phone because I was playing it in his class.
       A. set   **B.** confiscated   **C.** hold   **D.** sieze

    (4) Citizens of the EU can travel without _____ within the EU.
       A. limits   **B.** regulation   **C.** restriction   **D.** restrain

    (5) The company does not take proper fire _____.
       A. safeguard   **B.** security   **C.** precaution   **D.** caution

    (6) In a civilized community people like to _____ whenever they go to buy ticket or food.
       A. team up   **B.** push over   **C.** squeezed out   **D.** queue up

    (7) He refused to _____ them long-term credits.
       A. assign   **B.** grant   **C.** allow   **D.** award

    (8) She can _____ the advertisement pages of the newspapers in several minutes.
       A. scan   **B.** scrutinize   **C.** disregard   **D.** hop

    (9) His suggestion at the meeting _____ an interesting question.
       A. presents   **B.** poses   **C.** sets   **D.** lays

    (10) Preparedness _____ success.
       A. secure   **B.** ensures   **C.** assure   **D.** insure

Part C
Listening

Listen to the conversation about booking a flight seat. Decide whether the following statements are True (T) or False (F).

(1) Jim Brown is going to book a seat from London to New York on July 21.

(2) The seats on the flight leaving London airport at 17:30 in the afternoon are still available.

(3) The customer decides to book a seat on the 16:15 flight.

(4) The customer wants to book tickets for a round trip.

(5) The weight allowance is 20 kilos per traveler, including hand luggage.

New words and expressions

confirm	[kən'fɜːm]	*vt.*	确认；证实
extension	[ɪk'stenʃn]	*n.*	延长；电话分机
single	['sɪŋgl]	*n.*	单程票
terminal	['tɜːmɪnl]	*n.*	终点；航站楼
book a seat			预订座位；预订机票
check-in time			登记时间
fully booked			预订已满
local time			当地时间
Pan American Airways			泛美航空公司
return fare			回程票款
weight allowance			行李的限重

Part D
Translating

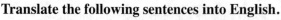

Translate the following sentences into English.

(1) 我想订一张 7 月 7 日从香港飞往纽约的单程商务舱机票。

(2) 请问我去日本旅行，该办哪些手续？

(3) 我下星期二将前往伦敦参加伦敦交易会。听说贵宾馆所有房间上周都订满了，但不知现在是否有取消的房间。如果有的话，我想订一间单人房。

(4) 我们要预订一个能够容纳 100 人的会议室，要有扩音设备、投影板或者屏幕，还备有电视机和录像机。

(5) 我能在酒店兑换一些钱吗？我想把一些美元兑换成当地货币。今天的兑换率是多少？

Part E
Writing skills: Graph description

　　商业报告以及文章中经常会有各种直观图表，包括饼状图（pie charts）、柱状图（bar graphs）、线形图（line charts）、表格（tables）等。这些图表能够简明、生动地比较和分析数据，解释和发现变化规律，解释抽象的概念等。

　　对图表进行描述可以分三步。首先，简要介绍该图表描述的对象。然后，对该图表所反映的总体趋势进行描述。描述整体变化趋势，只列出最重要、最有代表性、最核心的数据，切忌逐一列举数据。句式和词汇尽量多样化，不要使用单一、有限甚至是重复的句型和单词对图表进行描述。最后，如果需要的话可以做出结论，对主要发现进行归纳，不要引入新的观点，没有明确要求的情况下也不用解释图表反映的现象或发生的原因。

Example

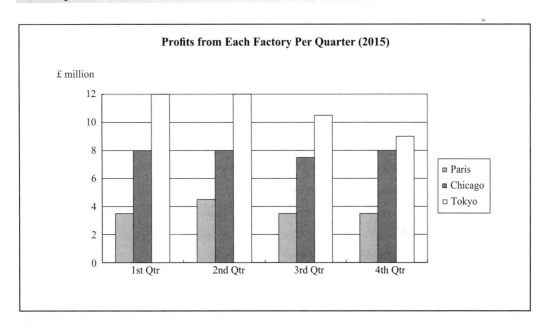

Number of Employees in Each Factory (2015)

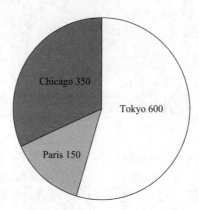

This report outlines the development of the profits in three plants, in Paris, Chicago and Tokyo, in 2021 and describes the staffing situation in each plant.

Tokyo, the company's largest factory, employed 600 people and reached profits of $12 million in the first quarter of 2021. The profits declined steadily, dropping to $9 million in the last quarter.

The factory in Chicago had a work force of 350 people. This made it the company's second largest plant. Profits remained almost unchanged at $8 million. In the third quarter however, they reached a low at $7.5 million.

The Paris factory's workforce comprised 150 people. Profits did not vary much and remained just over $3 million. Nevertheless, they peaked in the second quarter with earnings exceeding the $4 million level.

Case writing

Task: The graph below shows the turnover for three kinds of retail outlet, all owned by the same company, during a three-year period. Using the information from the graph, write a short report comparing the changes in turnover in the company's three types of outlet. Write in **120-140** words.

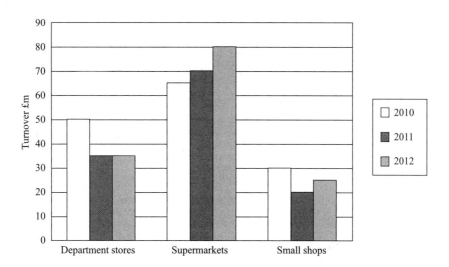

Part F
Further business story

Tips for Business Trips

Sometimes business people need to take business trips. Business travelers are primarily concerned with checking relevant travel **advisories**, acquiring the necessary travel **gear**, and traveling from point A to point B in the fastest and most convenient manner.

Traveling by train can be a reliable way to reach your destination while enjoying local scenery. Travelers **eschewing** a strict schedule may choose rail for its comforts and **amenities**. Eat a meal in the dining car, meet fellow travelers and get a good night's rest in a private sleeping cabin and a shower on an overnight ride. If time is **of the essence**, traveling by plane or car may be a more appropriate option.

Air travel is one of the most efficient means of transportation. Many people travel for business purposes every day, and air travel, via private jets and commercial airlines, accounts for a high percentage of business travel.

Air travel is frequently utilized by business travelers who need to travel long distances in a short amount of time. Airlines offer a convenient, efficient way to travel long distances for business or pleasure, and many companies are able to **accrue frequent flyer** *miles* which lower the cost of travel.

Upon arrival at his or her destination, the corporate traveler wants to quickly review *cultural highlights* and attractions offered in the area, then *lodge* at a comfortable hotel that provides tasty meals and standard business services. Arriving at the appointed conference or meeting fresh and well-rested is a key business travel objective.

Business travelers make up only 18% of travel volume in the United States, yet they contribute 33% of total domestic travel spending. There are a number of programs dedicated to serving this important market, from corporate travel agencies to online business travel websites. To take advantage of those programs and maximize efficiency, while reducing the cost of your business travels, follow these tips:

1) Plan ahead. Planning ahead is almost always the number-one way to get a better deal. From airline tickets to rental cars to hotel rooms, you'll likely pay less if you book in advance.

2) Use the Internet. Some websites offer discounted deals on hotels, car rentals, and plane tickets. Sometimes, though, the individual vendors may offer even lower rates. Before you book online, call the vendor directly to see if there's a lower rate. You can also search online for travel products catalogs as well as travel tips and articles.

3) Use your company's corporate travel manager or agency, if available. It can reduce the amount of time you spend planning your trip, and may reduce the cost if your company has negotiated deals with certain *vendors*.

4) Take advantage of travel group or association memberships. Being a member of an association could save you 10% on hotel rooms.

5) Consider booking a room on the executive level. While executive level rooms are often more expensive, the amenities they offer—from breakfast and afternoon *hors d'oeuvres* to *complimentary* use of the business center and meeting rooms—may outweigh the additional expense.

6) If you're going to be in one place for at least a week, consider *efficiency apartments or suite hotels* that charge weekly rates. Many efficiency-type hotels and apartments have small kitchens, allowing you to save money over restaurant meals.

7) If you need luggage or travel accessories for your business trip, you can find online a good selection of luggage and backpacks as well as briefcases and business travel *accessories*. There are many popular online sources of travel supplies.

8) When traveling overseas, remember that certain countries, particularly European countries in the *Schengen* area, require that your passport be valid for some months beyond your intended date of departure.

9) *Ditch* the excess baggage. Be particular about what you pack. Determine a clothing color and stick with that *palette*. Every pair of pants, skirt and shoes should be able to work with multiple outfits. Make sure you have everything you need for business

in your carry-on luggage (computer, presentation, documents, business appropriate clothes and shoes, *toiletries*, medication and device *chargers*) so even if your bag doesn't make it, you still have the essentials.

10) Print your *itinerary*. Your corporate travel department could send you itineraries or, maybe you've done the booking yourself. Either way, be sure to *compile* everything in one place. If your itinerary is stored in the *cloud*, it's not a bad idea to print a copy with phone numbers, e-mails and confirmation numbers. It might never *come in handy* until the power is out, your battery is dead and you really need to make a call.

11) Be prepared for the Expense Report. Between taxis, meals and accommodations, you'll probably spend a bit of money on this trip, whether it's on a company card or your own. Bring an envelope to keep all of your receipts together. Label each envelope with the date of the trip, client name and city (especially if you travel a lot on behalf of that client). You can even write notes on the envelope — airline, hotel, restaurants. Hang onto your receipts until you've been reimbursed.

Business trips will be full of fun if you had proper preparation! Bon voyage!

New words and expressions

accessory	*n.*	饰品；配件
accrue	*vt.*	获得；积累
advisory	*n.*	建议；注意事项
amenity	*n.*	方便，便利
charger	*n.*	充电器
cloud	*n.*	云端
compile	*vt.*	收集，汇集
complimentary	*adj.*	赠送的
ditch	*vt.*	丢弃
eschew	*vt.*	避免；避开；远避
gear	*n.*	衣服和装备
itinerary	*n.*	旅程，路线；旅行日程
lodge	*vi.*	寄宿；临时住宿
palette	*n.*	色系
reimburse	*vt.*	偿还；报销
Schengen	*n.*	申根
toiletry	*n.*	化妆品；化妆用具
vendor	*n.*	卖主；商家
come in handy		派得上用场
cultural highlight		文化名胜

efficiency apartment	有小厨房和卫生设备的小套公寓房间
frequent flyer miles	航空积分里程
hors d'oeuvre	开胃小吃；冷盘
of the essence	极其重要的
suite hotel	套房酒店

Critical thinking

Work in groups and discuss the following questions.

(1) For what reasons you will go on business travel?

(2) How to prepare for a business trip?

(3) What would you prepare when you plan to travel abroad?

Unit 10
Presenting
Products

Every year, businesses have to introduce lots of new products to the market in order to survive the competition and sustain development. In this unit you'll learn about how people present new products and deliver their marketing plan on new products.

Learning Objectives

* To list and define the words of presentations;
* To grasp the tips of doing presentations;
* To elicit details of product presentations;
* To familiarize with the structure of business reports.

Warm-up questions

(1) Can you recall some presentations you have ever made or done by others? Why are they impressive?

(2) What are the essentials for a successful product presentation?

Part A
General business vocabulary

1. **Match the words or phrases in the box with the following descriptions.**

> A. precaution   B. visual aid   C. bibliography   D. appendix
>
> E. promptu   F. format   G. retail outlet   H. flip chart
>
> I. production capacity   J. presentation

(1) Volume of products that can be generated by a production plant or enterprise in a given period by using current resources.

(2) A measure taken beforehand to prevent harm or secure goods.

(3) A descriptive or persuasive account of something (as by a salesman of a product).

(4) Made or done without previous thought or preparation.

(5) An instructional device (as a chart, map, or model) that appeals chiefly to vision; especially, an educational motion picture or filmstrip.

(6) A stationery item consisting of a pad of large paper sheets. It is typically fixed to the upper edge of a whiteboard, typically supported on a tripod or four-legged easel.

(7) A store that sells smaller quantities of products or services to the general public. Such business will typically buy goods directly from manufacturers or wholesale suppliers at a volume discount and will then mark them up in price for sale to end consumers.

(8) The way in which something is sized, arranged, or organized.

(9) The history, identification, or description of writings or publications, usually appear at the end of the writings.

(10) Supplementary material usually attached at the end of a piece of writing.

2.   Listen to the conversations and answer the questions.

(1) What are the reasons for the fabric to be wear-resisting?

(2) How can the customer order only the products with the lighter color?

(3) What is the difference between the latest product and the usual one?

(4) What is the characteristic of the wool carpet?

(5) When did the new product appear in the market?

(6) What is the medicine for?

(7) Why is it practical for family use?

(8) What should you do if it sprays into your eyes?

Part B
Reading

Elements of Doing Good Presentation

[1] Presentation refers to a short talk by one person to a group of people introducing and describing a particular subject such a new product, company figures or a proposed advertising campaign in business field. A successful presentation is one of the most effective ways of communicating your message. It is widely used in many fields in the world today. Believe it or not, preparation is a better ***determinant*** of presentation success than knowledge, experience or even talent. The best presenter is almost always the presenter who is the most prepared. Thorough preparation adds to the speaker's self-confidence and reduces the chances of nervousness.

[2] Following are the commonly recognized main elements involved in preparing and delivering an effective presentation:

[3] Sell the idea. You must keep in mind that you are selling something to your audience, whether it is a product, a project, an idea, a strategy, concept or anything else. The primary goal of your presentation must be to convince the audience that they should "buy".

[4] Tell a ***compelling*** story. Your presentation of the idea and its ***ramifications*** must be so thorough, attractive and convincing that the audience is eager to buy into what you're selling. Basically, you're ***capturing*** their imagination.

[5] Be ***concise***. State your ideas, goals, and benefits received in a ***crisp***, brief and meaningful manner. Use relevant facts and figures that ***drive home*** the key message that you're trying to ***get across to*** your audience.

[6] ***Mode*** of Delivery. Several modes of delivery are available to speakers—***impromptu***,

textual, and *memorization*. When you are asked to speak without any notice, you make an impromptu speech (sometimes called an *extemporaneous* speech). Take a few moments to gather your thoughts before speaking and avoid *rambling* by including an introduction, a body, and a closing. When making a textual presentation, you read from a written copy of your speech, from an outline, or from note cards. Reading a speech is not recommended unless the material is highly technical. Even then, maintaining *eye contact* is essential. Speaking from an outline or notes is effective because you can maintain eye contact while referring to notes to make sure you cover major points. Memorizing an entire speech is not recommended because you may forget lines or become *flustered*. Also, a memorized speech often sounds *stilted* and formal. Memorizing a quotation or opening or closing remarks, however, can be effective.

[7] Key objectives. What do you want to communicate to an audience? Answering this question will help you determine the objective of your presentation. State the purpose, scope and objectives of the presentation in a clear, concise manner. This can include both qualitative and quantitative elements.

[8] Plan. Tell the story on how to achieve your objectives (i.e. what activities or tasks need to be done). This is where you identify and describe your strategy (i.e. What, When, Where, How).

[9] Supporting evidence. Support the main body with relevant *business charts* to illustrate and highlight key figures. Use relevant facts to support your story. *Visual aids* should be used to emphasize, explain, or illustrate points of your presentation. *Transparencies*, *flip charts*, chalkboards or whiteboards, slides, and computer presentations are examples of visual aids.

[10] Call to action. Creating a sense of urgency for the approval of what you're presenting *ASAP*, and instilling a sense of loss if your idea does not proceed beyond this point.

New words and expressions

ASAP		*abbr.*	尽快（as soon as possible）
capture	['kæptʃə]	*vt.*	捕获
compelling	[kəm'pelɪŋ]	*adj.*	引人注目的，强有力的
concise	[kən'saɪs]	*adj.*	简洁的
crisp	[krɪsp]	*adj.*	脆的，新鲜的
determinant	[dɪ'tɜ:mɪnənt]	*n.*	决定因素
		adj.	决定性的
extemporaneous	[ɪk͵stempə'reɪnɪəs]	*adj.*	即席的
fluster	['flʌstə]	*vt.*	使慌张，使激动
impromptu	[ɪm'prɒmtju:]	*n.*	即席演出
		adj.	即席的
		adv.	即席地

memorization	[ˌmemərɪ'zeʃn]	*n.*	记住
mode	[məʊd]	*n.*	模式，方式
ramble	['ræmbl]	*vi.*	漫步，漫谈
ramification	[ˌræmɪfɪ'keɪʃn]	*n.*	衍生物，分支
stilted	['stɪltɪd]	*adj.*	呆板的
textual	['tekstjʊəl]	*adj.*	本文的，按原文的
transparency	[træn'spærnsɪ]	*n.*	幻灯片
business charts			业务图表
drive home			使人理解
eye contact			眼神交流
flip charts			活动挂图
get across to			让……听懂
visual aids			视觉工具

Reading comprehension

1. Work in pairs and discuss whether the following statements are True (T) or False (F).

(1) An excellent presentation is the top guarantee for your success of business.

(2) The importance of preparation for the success of presentation is second only to your rich knowledge on the project.

(3) The preparation and delivery of an effective presentation involved at least 8 elements.

(4) The purpose of telling an attractive story is to capture your clients' imagination.

(5) Deliver your statement in a crisp and beautiful way to make your clients feel at home.

2. Choose the best answers to explain the meanings of the underlined words.

(1) I'd love to hear about other current, <u>impressive</u> projects, and your thoughts on how you see those projects changing in the near future.
  A. complicated   **B.** competitive   **C.** compelling   **D.** compatible

(2) Electronic information crimes are <u>deviation</u> from modern high-technology development.
  A. ramification   **B.** rectification   **C.** rambling   **D.** rampart

(3) "I was trying to <u>seize</u> the feeling of the movement," he explained.
  A. puncture   **B.** capture   **C.** rapture   **D.** nurture

(4) Be sure to make it clear and <u>brief</u> and avoid long-windedness.
  A. concise   **B.** converse   **C.** reverse   **D.** concerned

(5) This is the message that we want to <u>deliver</u> to the public.
  A. get over   **B.** come across   **C.** move forward   **D.** get across

(6) At one point someone gets up and performs an <u>extemporaneous</u> Balkan dance.

    A. improper   **B.** impromptu   **C.** impossible   **D.** incorporate

(7) The moors, where you <u>roam</u> with him, are much nicer, and Thrushcross Park is the finest place in the world.

    A. resist   **B.** respect   **C.** remember   **D.** ramble

(8) Our first academic visit, to the History Department of Wuhan University, sticks in my mind for its very <u>stiff</u> and tense nature.

    A. ruled   **B.** stilted   **C.** still   **D.** moved

(9) Greeks mastered the principle of imagination and association to <u>recite</u> everything.

    A. recognize   **B.** realize   **C.** mention   **D.** memorize

(10) Another <u>key</u> factor that must be observed by you are interactions and reactions.

    A. decline   **B.** delimitation   **C.** determinant   **D.** determination

Part C
Listening

Listen to the conversation about the newly launched product "Viscal", and decide whether the following statements are True (T) or False (F).

(1) Viscal 2020 is the latest video game product.

(2) The speaker majorly talked about the four P's about the new product.

(3) The product totally consists of four elements.

(4) There will be an audio delay of about 2 seconds.

(5) There is not spot goods yet when the speaker was presenting the product.

New words and expressions

commission	[kə'mɪʃn]	*n.*	委员会，委任
mock-up	['mɒkʌp]	*n.*	实物模型
outlet	['aʊtlet]	*n.*	销路，批发商店
penetration	[penɪ'treɪʃn]	*n.*	渗透，突破
subscriber	[səb'skraɪbə]	*n.*	订阅者，用户
terminal	['tɜːmɪnl]	*n.*	终端；*adj.* 末端的
transmitter	[trænz'mɪtə]	*n.*	发送器；由……构成

Part D
Translating

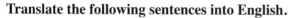

Translate the following sentences into English.

(1) 我们产品的质量与其他供应商的一样好，而价格却没有他们的高。

(2) 宣传信息必须有冲击力，有足够的说服力，以激发客户采取行动。

(3) 我们的产品有着最高的性价比，有稳定的消费群体。

(4) 我公司是一家融科、工、贸于一体的跨地区、跨行业、跨所有制的（集团）公司。

(5) 当你使用视觉辅助进行展示时，观众的注意力会被吸引，你应该随即进行解释说明。

Part E
Writing skills: Business report

写作提示

　　商务报告是一种应用广泛的文体。它通常是根据上司的要求，由下级向上级呈报。报告分为书面和口头报告两种形式。相比之下，书面报告具有"永久性记载"的特点，便于日后查阅和参考。口头报告容易被人遗忘，且经过众人之口之后其细节还有可能被歪曲。

　　书面报告可以用书信形式撰写，也可以用报告形式撰写。报告的篇幅没有限制，根据实际需要可长可短。写报告要思路清晰，文字简洁有说服力。报告的目的是发现问题、分析问题和解决问题。其作用是通报情况、传递信息、提出建议、为正确的决策提供可靠的依据，是保证各方面工作顺利进行的前提。由此可见，掌握报告的写作对于从事商务活动的业务工作人员来说非常重要。

　　书面报告的构成：

　　标题（**Title**）。标题是文章的一个组成部分。写作时要认真拟定题目，力求简洁、明确地表达报告主题，切忌华而不实，弄巧成拙。

　　引言（**Introduction**）。引言又称导言或内容提要，写法可根据报告的具体内容、类型和读者对象而定。引言要简明扼要，条例清晰，具有概括性。引言具有导读效果，为理解报告打下基础，并增强报告的真实感、强调核心内容，使读者在读正文前，先有一个总体上的印象。若是分析报告，还应该在引言里提出问题提示结论。但也有的报告没有引言，开门见山地表述中心内容。

　　正文（**Body**）。正文是报告的主体部分，着重反映调查分析的成果，包括典型的事例、确凿的数据、合理的分析、明确的判断以及令人信服的结论等。该部分的内容应该十分详尽、具体。因此段落既要条理清晰，又要相互联系，相互照应。

结语（**Conclusion**）。结语是上述调研报告陈述内容的结论。通过对全文进行总结，深化主题并提出问题、引发思考，与引言相照应。从内容的完整性和严密性来看，报告通常需要一个结语。结语部分根据报告的不同类型而定。

署名和日期（**Date and Signature**）。署名和日期的位置比较灵活。

写书面报告的注意事项：

1）语句精练，准确；

2）句子意思连贯，详细得当，层次分明；

3）客观地反映事物的发展规律内在联系，不要有任何个人的偏见和夸大的语言；

4）借助于表格、图表、照片等缩短报告的篇幅，讲明报告的内容，增强文章的可读性，同时为读者节约时间。

Example

To: All the board directors
From: Chief executive
Date: May 9, 2020
Subject: On the reinvest of this year's profit

Introduction

This report sets out to examine how the company should reinvest this year's profits.

Alternatives

The areas under consideration are:

1) the purchase of new computers;

2) the provision of language training courses;

3) the payment of special bonuses.

Evaluations

New computers: The majority of company computers are quite new and fast enough to handle the work done on them. Consequently, new computers would not be recommended.

Language training courses: The company aims to increase exports, particularly in Spain and France. Therefore, language training course would be an excellent idea for those employees who deal with business partners and customers overseas. In addition, training courses would increase motivation; staff would enjoy the lessons and perceive that the company is investing in them. Therefore, language training would be an option.

Special bonus payment: Although special bonus payments would have a beneficial impact on motivation, they would have no direct effect on the company's operations. There are also potential problems concerning the selection of staff eligible for the payments and the setting of a precedent for future payments, therefore bonus payments would not be advisable.

Conclusion

1) Purchasing new computer is not necessary at present.

2) Special bonus payment may not be advisable for now.

3) Language training courses are good for both company's operation and employee's motivation.

Recommendation

It is felt that the best solution for both the company and staff would be to invest in language training. It is suggested that the company should organize courses in French and Spainish.

Those employees who have contact with partners should be assured of places but other interested members of staff should also be allowed to attend.

Case writing

Task: Suppose that your managing director asks you to investigate on health and safety provisions in the office. The following is the notes you have taken down. Write a report based on it.

Your notes:

My task were: 1) to speak to office managers and union representatives about how accident or job-related illness happened, and 2) to make recommendation on how best to improve the situation.

Results of study of all reported accidents of the past year.

Three main causes

√ faulty equipment

√ safety regulations not followed

√ health / safety procedures being ignored

Study some job-related illness reported.

Also had meetings with union reps and office managers about what to do.

Make recommendations/proposals.

Write in about **120-140** words.

Part F
Further business story

How to Plan Reports

Types of reports

A report is a document that provides the facts about a specific situation or problem for consideration by a specific group of people. Reports are business tools that enable managers to make decisions or solve problems. Reports can be classified according to their style, purpose, and *format*.

The two styles of reports are formal and informal. Formal reports generally are long, analytical, and *impersonal*. A formal report often contains *preliminary* parts such as a title page, an executive summary, and a table of contents, as well as *supplementary* parts such as a *bibliography* and an *appendix*. An example of a formal report is a company's annual report to stockholders or a report to a government regulatory agency. Another example is an external proposal, a report that analyzes a problem and recommends a solution to people outside the writer's company.

Informal reports are shorter than formal reports and are written in a less formal style. Unlike formal reports, informal reports generally have no preliminary or supplementary parts because they usually are concerned with everyday matters that require little background. In addition, an informal report is organized differently from a formal report. A sales report is an example of an informal report. In sales report, the writer summarizes sales for a specific period. Another type of informal report, an internal proposal (also known as a *justification report*), is used to analyze an internal problem and recommend a solution.

Based on purpose, reports can be either information or analytical. Informational reports present information, so they include very little analysis. For example, a bank manager may ask the head cashier to prepare an informational report about the average number and value of money orders sold each day. The components of an informational report are the topics or the areas investigated. Analytical reports analyze a problem, present facts, draw conclusions, and make recommendations. *In contrast* to an informational report, which just presents the facts, an analytical report also suggests what might be done to solve the problem. The components of an analytical report are the probable causes and solutions of the problems.

Informal reports can be written in several different formats, including memo, letter and *manuscript* formats. Formal reports are longer and more complex than informal reports, so they are written in manuscript format.

Steps in planning reports

Before writing a report, you must do some preliminary work. Even if you are simply reporting facts, you must gather those facts and then arrange them in an easy-to-follow, logical sequence. When planning a report, you should (1) identify the problem; (2) decide on areas to investigate; (3) determine the scope; (4) plan the research; (5) develop a preliminary outline; (6) collect the data; and (7) analyze the data, draw conclusions, and make recommendations.

The first step is to identify the problem to be studied and the objective of the report. As in planning letters and memos, determine why you are writing the report and what you hope to accomplish. Prepare a written statement of the problem you will analyze in your report. Depending on the *preferences* of your company and your supervisor, this statement may be expressed as an infinitive phrase, as a question, or as a statement.

Your next step is to decide exactly what to investigate. Only after you understand the problem and the *scope* of the investigation can you plan your research and identify specific areas to investigate. Scope refers to the boundaries of the report—what will be included and excluded. For example, a report about the use of computers in all departments will require more research and have a wider scope than a report that examines computer use in just two departments.

Once you know the scope of your report, develop a plan for getting the facts you need. List the questions that need answers and execute the steps you need to find those answers. Also consider how much time and money you have. Then develop a schedule for collecting the data, analyzing the results, and writing and finishing the report on time.

Now you are ready to prepare a preliminary outline to organize the facts you uncover in your research. This preliminary outline will likely differ from the final outline you use to write your report. The preliminary outline is simply a way of organizing the topic you decided to investigate.

When outlining analytical reports, you can organize the facts in one of two ways. One method is to use a *hypothesis*, a possible cause or explanation of the problem. The second method is to use *alternatives*. In the method with hypothesis, phrase each possible outline shows two hypotheses for a drop in auto sales. Under each hypothesis are the questions that must be answered to prove or disprove the hypothesis. For example, if the hypothesis is that our prices are too high, then the questions that should be answered are such as (1) What are our prices? (2) What are our competitors' prices? (3) How important is price to our customers? To evaluate alternative solutions to a problem, arrange your preliminary outline according to the relative merits of each alternative. For example, to determine where in your school building to install new computers, one alternative is to research the number of courses in each subject that use computers. Another alternative is to research the number of students enrolled in each course that uses computers.

The next step in planning a report is to perform research by collecting appropriate data. Two sources of data are available—primary and secondary. Primary research involves gathering fresh, new data, whereas secondary research involves locating data that already has been gathered and reported. If the facts you need are not available in books, magazines, or other sources, you may need to conduct primary research. To conduct this type of research, you might talk with experts, customers, or suppliers. Observe what happens in a particular situation, or experiment to see what works. On the other hand, research completed by others also can be useful. Consult books, periodicals, other reports, available at many libraries, often offer a more thorough search of the literature than may be available in printed form in the library. As you conduct your research, you will need a method of identifying your sources. You can do this by preparing a bibliography card for every source. These cards provide the details for the bibliography that the formal report will include.

Unless you have been asked to provide only an informational report, the last step in preparing to write a report is to analyze the results, draw conclusions, and make recommendations. Once you have your research results—the data—look for logical links between facts and figures. If you are working with numerical data, compare and contrast figures. Then organize the material in a way that helps the reader. For example, if you researched the high turnover rate of production supervisors in your manufacturing company, you might put the data into three categories: salaries of different supervisory jobs in the company, salaries offered by competing manufactures, and the number and kinds of promotions supervisors have received at each job level. After you have analyzed the data, you may arrive at a conclusion, an opinion based on *interpretation* of data. Here's a possible conclusion for the study of high turnover among production supervisors: Production supervisors in our company have limited advancement opportunities. Include recommendations in a report if you have been asked to do so. A recommendation offers suggestions of what should be done. Recommendations should be related to conclusions, as in the following: I ***recommend*** that supervisory positions within our company be reorganized to provide opportunities for career advancement.

New words and expressions

alternative	*n.*	替换物
appendix	*n.*	附录
bibliography	*n.*	参考书目
format	*n.*	版式
hypothesis	*n.*	假设，假说
impersonal	*adj.*	客观的
interpretation	*n.*	解释
manuscript	*n.*	手稿
preference	*n.*	偏爱
preliminary	*adj.*	初步的
recommend	*v.*	推荐
scope	*n.*	范围
supplementary	*adj.*	补充的
in contrast to		与……形成对照
justification report		论证报告

Critical thinking

Work in groups and discuss the following questions.

(1) Why are reports classified according to style, purpose, and format?

(2) Do findings, conclusions, and recommendations differ? If so, how?

(3) Is there a process that would help reports to be consistent?

Unit 11

Logistics

Logistics is generally the detailed organization and implementation of a complex operation. In a general business sense, logistics is the management of the flow of things between the point of origin and the point of consumption in order to meet requirements of customers or corporations.

Learning objectives

* To explain terms of logistics;
* To discuss logistics planning process;
* To grasp the gist of a listening text about logistics;
* To understand the layout of a proposal.

Warm-up

(1) What are the important factors when logistics are mentioned?

(2) What problems does a logistic company probably face at present?

Part A
General business vocabulary

1. **Match the words in the box with the following descriptions.**

> A. budget   B. end-user   C. requisition   D. consignment
>
> E. tender   F. consignee   G. logistics   H. containerization
>
> I. supplier   J. forwarder

(1) The person uses a particular product, rather than the people who make or develop it.

(2) It is a company or a person that provides a particular product.

(3) The purpose of this action is to make a formal offer to do a job or provide goods or services for a particular price.

(4) It is a quantity of goods that are sent somewhere, especially in order to be sold.

(5) The money is available to an organization or person, or a plan of how it will be spent.

(6) It is an official, usually written, demand for especially the use of property or materials by an army in wartime or by certain people in an emergency.

(7) It is the action of putting goods into standard sized containers in order to move them by road, rail, or ship.

(8) The person is entitled to take the delivery of the goods.

(9) A company takes goods somewhere or arranges for them to be taken there by other companies.

(10) The practical arrangements are needed in order to make a plan that involves a lot of people and equipment successful.

2. Listen to the conversations and answer the questions.

(1) Why does the company delay shipping?

(2) What is the ultimate unloading port?

(3) How long can the first speaker wait for the order?

(4) Why does the second speaker agree to transshipment at last?

(5) According to the second speaker, who should take responsibility for the packing breakage?

(6) What's the first speaker's idea of shipment in the middle of October?

(7) How can the second speaker prove that the first speaker used second-hand bags for the last shipment?

(8) What should the first speaker do firstly when he or she finds a shortage in the shipment?

Part B
Reading

Logistics

[1] Logistics is defined as the process of planning, implementing and controlling the efficient and cost-effective flow and storage of raw materials, goods, equipment and personnel from the point of origin until the completion of an activity, in accordance with **end-user**'s requirements.

[2] In its broadest sense, logistics includes all the elements that constitute a delivery **infrastructure**, however, in this context, focus will be on the aspects of logistics that are relevant to the **procurement process**.

Logistics planning process

[3] Proper logistics planning **entails** considering logistical aspects throughout the various stages of the procurement process. It contributes to efficient procurement processes, and reduces the risk of **incurring** problems that may lead to additional costs and delay.

[4] Logistics planning starts at the **needs assessment** phase of procurement by considering the desired result of the **requisitioner** and the end-user and from there working backwards to determine what will lead to a successful completion of the activity. Ideally this process should begin even before the **requisition** is placed, through close cooperation and efficient

communication between the operational unit requesting the purchase and procurement officers. [5] The aspects of logistics planning that should be considered during the various stages of the procurement process are detailed below:

1) Understanding the operational context of the required product, and, if possible, assist in developing specifications suitable to local conditions.

2) Evaluating the procurement activity and the time and financial resources available in order to determine urgency of the requirement. Urgency may determine location of the purchase and thereby also the mode of transport.

3) Determining the type of sourcing. Goods may be purchased locally/regionally or internationally or through established *LTAs*. These options should be considered when determining whether to purchase, and how and where to purchase, the required product, in order to meet end-user's needs in a timely and cost efficient manner.

4) Determining which markets are best positioned to respond to the end-user's delivery requirements by evaluating total delivered costs as well as *lead times*, in addition to *conformity* with technical criteria.

5) Reviewing the delivery and transport requirements, as well as the budget, and ensuring that they are complete and realistic. The cost of transportation is a significant component in the cost of goods *procured* and delivered to the designated site.

6) Determining and comparing total lead time, including logistics activities. Different logistics corridors incur different costs, but also have an impact on total lead times.

7) Determining the most cost effective means of contracting transport, i.e. from the supplier included in the purchase order, or contracted to independent freight *forwarder*. Some organizations also allow transportation with their own resources.

8) *Tendering* for freight services, if determined under aspect number 6 listed above, and checking availability and competitiveness of an LTA for freight services.

9) Insuring a *consignment* in accordance with the policy of the organization.

10) Ensuring that shipping documents received from the supplier and freight forwarder are complete and accurate and that the *consignee* has received their set.

11) Ensuring that necessary arrangements are in place to clear cargo on arrival. Depending upon the procedures in the country, the consignee could be responsible for custom clearance of the goods.

12) Obtaining acknowledgement from consignee that the shipment has been received in good order.

Throughout this process, the requisitioner and/or end-user should be kept informed of expected and actual delivery dates in order for them to account for it in their local planning.

Logistics requirements for goods

[6] The following logistical requirements should be considered for the shipment of goods:

- packing and *containerization*;
- packing and shipping instructions;
- labeling and shipping marks;
- modes of transportation;
- forwarding agents;
- *incoterms*;
- insurance during transportation;
- shipping documents;
- receipt of consignment.

Restrictions on the export or import of goods

[7] Exporting countries may restrict the shipment of certain classes of goods to certain countries or ban their export altogether. Equipment that has a dual civilian/military use or *high-end* computer and telecommunications technology are commonly considered. The procurement officer should be aware of these restrictions so that lead time required for authorization can be calculated and the sourcing strategy modified if necessary.

[8] Importing countries may also impose restrictions. Telecommunications equipment and *pharmaceuticals* typically require *prior authorization* from the concerned ministry who will issue a licence. Other equipment, such as used vehicles older than a certain age, may be banned outright. Some countries ban goods of certain origins for political reasons. Obtaining permits is generally a *protracted* exercise. The receiving office must confirm that it is in hand before the supplier is authorized to ship the goods. The likely consequence of shipping without the permit is that the receiver will be required to pay the cost of storage in the port and applicable liner charges until the authorization is issued. There is also the considerable risk that the cargo will *deteriorate* or go missing during this period. There are also UN restrictions for countries. For more information please refer to the UN Committee on Sanctions web-page.

New words and expressions

conformity	[kən'fɔːmɪtɪ]	*n.*	一致，适合
consignee	[ˌkɒnsaɪ'niː]	*n.*	收件人；受托者
consignment	[kən'saɪnm(ə)nt]	*n.*	委托；托付物
containerization	[kən,tenərɪ'zeʃən]	*n.*	集装箱化
deteriorate	[dɪ'tɪərɪəreɪt]	*vi.*	恶化
end-user	['endˌjuːzə]	*n.*	终端用户

entail	[ɪn'teɪl]	vt.	必需；蕴含
forwarder	['fɔːwədə]	n.	运送者；货运代理
high-end	['haɪ-end]	adj.	高端的
incoterms	['ɪnkəʊˌtɜːmz]	abbr.	国际贸易术语（International Commercial Terms）
incur	[ɪn'kɜː]	vt.	引发
infrastructure	['ɪnfrəstrʌktʃə]	n.	基础设施
pharmaceutical	[ˌfɑːmə'suːtɪkl]	n.	药物
procure	[prəkjuə]	vt.	获得
protracted	[prə'træktɪd]	adj.	拖延的
requisitioner	[ˌrekwɪ'zɪʃnə]	n.	申购人
requisition	[ˌrekwɪ'zɪʃn]	n.	要求；申请书
tender	['tendə]	vi.	投标
lead time			订货至交货的时间
LTA (Land Transport Authority)			陆路交通管理局
need assessment			需求评估
prior authorization			事先核准
procurement process			采购流程

Reading comprehension

1. **Work in pairs and discuss the following questions according to the passage.**

   (1) What is logistics?

   (2) What is proper logistics planning involved in?

   (3) What should be taken into consideration for the shipment of goods?

   (4) What kind of goods is usually restricted to export and import?

   (5) What are possible outcomes of shipping restricted goods without permit?

2. **Choose the best answers to explain the meaning of the underlined words.**

   (1) Most people recognize the benefits of individuality, but the fact is that personal economic success requires underlined conformity.

   A. harmony   B. confinement   C. conversation   D. conclusion

   (2) Obviously, if the city is to procure food from the countryside it must have something of value to give in exchange.

   A. process   B. profit   C. profile   D. acquire

   (3) Portraits of people will draw readers' attention, especially if the images are relevant and tell a story.

   A. affirmative   B. appropriate.   C. reactive   D. reluctant

(4) The company has <u>incurred</u> huge losses over the past three years.
  A. occurred   B. recurred   C. contracted   D. conquered

(5) With so much at stake and such large companies involved, we are surely about to witness a long and <u>protracted</u> battle.
  A. contracted   B. interacted   C. reacted   D. prolonged

(6) He wanted to be on time for work, so he wrote down what that would <u>entail</u>: waking up, showering, dressing, preparing breakfast, eating, driving, parking and buying coffee—all before 9 am.
  A. tail   B. implicate   C. retail   D. detail

(7) The changes to the national health system will be <u>implemented</u> next year.
  A. achieved   B. complimented   C. competed   D. inspired

(8) She was taken into hospital last week when her condition suddenly <u>deteriorated</u>.
  A. established   B. finished   C. worsened   D. aggregated

(9) They had to refuse the dinner invitation because of a <u>prior</u> engagement.
  A. related   B. previous   C. creative   D. efficient

(10) I am recommending to my clients that they do not <u>purchase</u> another apartment unless their home sells first.
  A. attack   B. attract   C. standardize   D. buy

Part C
Listening

Listen to an Interview with Evergreen Group, Chairman Dr. Y. F. Chang. Decide whether the following statements are True (T) or False (F).

(1) The Evergreen Group developed in the year 1975 and currently operates as the world's fourth largest containerized-freight shipping company.

(2) When entering the liner business, Dr. Y. F. Chang had ordered P-type vessels instead of S-type which made his great success.

(3) In the year 1975, it was more liberal to start an independent liner container service in America.

(4) From Chang's perspective, his competitors felt nothing about his success and they accounted his success for his good luck.

(5) People can talk about logistics without mentioning shipping, because shipping doesn't play an important role at that time based on Chang's idea.

New words and expressions

acrimony	['ækrɪmənɪ]	n.	尖刻
bellwether	['belweðə]	n.	前导；领导者
blackball	['blækbɔːl]	vt.	排斥；投反对票
buzzword	['bʌzwɜːd]	n.	流行词
carrier	['kærɪə]	n.	运货人；货运公司
cartel	[kɑː'tel]	n.	企业联合；垄断联盟
commence	[kə'mens]	vt.	开始；着手
compliant	[kəm'plaɪənt]	adj.	顺从的；服从的
confluence	['kɒnfluəns]	n.	（人或物的）聚集
conglomerate	[kən'glɒmrət]	n.	企业集团
culprit	['kʌlprɪt]	n.	犯人，罪犯
diversification	[daɪˌvɜːsɪfɪ'keɪʃən]	n.	多样化；变化
façade	[fə'sɑːd]	n.	外观；表面
laden	['leɪdn]	adj.	负载的；装满的
momentous	[məʊ'mentəs]	adj.	重要的；重大的
mothball	['mɒθbɔːl]	vt.	封存
multifaceted	[mʌltɪ'fæsɪtɪd]	adj.	多层面的
non-compensatory	['nɒnˌkɒmpen'seɪtərɪ]	adj.	非补偿的，非赔偿的
peeved	[piːvd]	adj.	恼怒的；不高兴的
scramble	['skræmbl]	vt.	争夺，竞争
solidarity	[ˌsɒlɪ'dærɪtɪ]	n.	团结，团结一致
stigma	['stɪgmə]	n.	烙印；特征
second-to-none			首屈一指

Part D
Translating

Translate the following sentences into English.

(1) 从最广义上来说，物流包括构成货物递送基础设施的所有元素。

(2) 现代物流需要日益复杂的信息、通信以及在今天的商业环境内所必备的控制体系。

(3) 通过物流过程，原料被送往工业国家并通过他们的制造能力转化为成品，制造好的成品又被运送至消费者。

(4) 合理的物流规划需要考虑物流的方方面面，它们贯穿于整个采购过程的不同阶段。

(5) 某货物可能会被出口国限制装运到某些国家或被完全禁止其出口。

(6) 在供应商授权发货之前，接收方必须确认许可证正在办理之中。

Part E
Writing skills: Proposal

写作提示

商业建议书（Proposal）是常见的商务写作形式之一，它与商务报告（Report）相似，又不同于报告。商务建议书关注的是未来，重点在于建议讨论的内容，形式可以是备忘录或是电子邮件等；而商务报告是就有关具体问题或事件做信息陈述。

商务建议书大多由下级写给上级，因此要采用正式的语言。在撰写的过程中，可以适当多地使用被动语态、复杂词汇、长句等。在写作之前必须明确以下问题：写作目的是什么？写作对象是谁？写作对象已知什么？想要了解什么？采用什么样的语气来写？

商务建议书的结构（Layout）：

1. Proposal

这部分需要根据题目要求填写，商务建议书的题目一般为 *Proposal on...*

2. Introduction

在该部分中，需要指出建议书的目的。

可以套用的句型：

The purpose /objective / aim of the proposal is to...

This proposal aims to...

3. Findings

在本部分，需要列出主要发现，每一条都应该是信息点的内容。

4. Conclusion

在本部分，需要陈述结论，可以套用以下句型：

According to the findings above, it can be concluded that...

Therefore, it can be concluded that...

5. Recommendation

可以直接陈述结论，需要注意的是 *recommendation* 和 *recommend* 后面要接虚拟语气。

可以采用的句型：

It is recommended that...

Based on the analysis above, we recommend that...

如果需要进一步展开，可以描述一下建议实施后可预期的进展或结果，可以用 *so that...* 或者 *thus...* 句型来补充说明。

需要注意的是，在一些商务建议书中，很难将某个或某些信息点归结到某一个小标题下，此时可以舍弃上面的 Proposal 结构，直接采用个性化的小标题（具体见下例）。

Example

Introduction

This proposal aims to analyze the needs for the new staff and propose ways of recruitment.

Reasons for recruitment

Since we have to deal with the large new order, recruiting new staff clearly becomes necessary. Otherwise, we may not meet the deadline.

Number of staff needed

Altogether we need ten more staff. Based on analysis of the workload of each staff, ten more staff will greatly improve the working efficiency.

Necessary skills and experiences

Candidates are required to be proficient in English, since they must deal with clients from North America. Moreover, they should possess at least one-year experience on marketing because persuading skills are necessary, especially when they communicate with potential customers.

Recruiting methods

To get the best candidates, we need resort to some headhunters since they own "talent pools". This is obviously an effective way.

Length of labor contract

To lower the turnover rate, we should sign a two-year contract with staff rather than the usual one-year term. The more career safety we offer, the more efficiency they yield.

Case writing

Task: Write a proposal based on the following directions:

* The manufacturer you work for is looking for an advertising agency to promote its products. Your line manager has asked you to write a proposal recommending a suitable agency.
* Look at the information below, on which you have already made some handwritten notes.
* Then using all your handwritten notes, write a proposal for your line manager.
  Write in about **120-140** words.

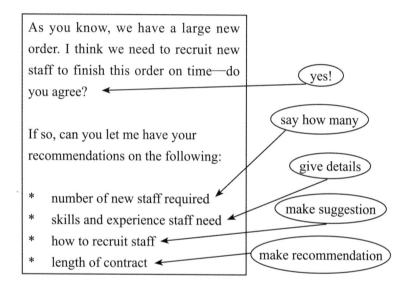

Part F
Further business story

DHL: A Leader in Global Logistics

DHL Global *Forwarding*, the division of DHL which handles heavy freight by air, sea or land, is hosting a large conference in Malta today. Its CEO for Europe, Middle East and Africa, Thomas Nieszner, tells *The Times* in an interview that DHL has grown over the past 40 years from a company of three people to a leader in global logistics.

"The DHL success story started back in 1969 in San Francisco with a revolutionary *entrepreneurial* idea. The pioneering spirit and focus on customer needs created a whole new industry and these are still among the most important features of our DHL brand,"

Mr. Nieszner says.

Over the years, the DHL network grew ever larger, gradually reaching out to new customers in every corner of the world. At the same time, the marketplace developed and became more complex, so DHL adapted to meet the changing needs of its customers—both at global and local level. "Today, DHL's international network links more than 220 countries and territories worldwide. DHL also offers *unparalleled expertise* in express, air and ocean freight, *overland* transport, contract logistics solutions as well as international mail services. From 1969 until today, the approach and dedication has remained the same. Our success has always been based around delivering excellent service for our customers."

"In recent years, DHL has grown into the global *umbrella brand* for our global mail, express, freight, global forwarding and supply chain solutions. These *segments* operate under the control of their own divisional headquarters. DHL Global Forwarding is the global leader in the air and ocean freight markets. We transport goods and merchandise to an agreed destination, at a customer specific agreed delivery time and price, providing customized solutions for major logistics projects, as well as comprehensive customs services. We're the global leader in Air freight, carrying 12% of the total worldwide market, more than twice as much as the second biggest organization."

Mr. Nieszner explains that Deutsche Post DHL has published a report entitled *Delivering Tomorrow—Customer Needs in 2020 and Beyond* which provides a number of expert opinions and analyses on issues such as globalization, economy, technology, logistics, environment and society. The study reveals future trends in these areas up to the year 2020 and even beyond. By carrying out this study, the mail and logistics group has created an *orientation* guide for possible future *scenarios*.

"With the DHL Innovation Centre, which is unique in the logistics field, a place has been created where DHL Solutions and Innovations combined capacity for innovation is made *tangible* and brought to life for visitors. In the DHL Innovation Centre, specialists from the academic, industrial and technological fields exchange their knowledge and talk about advanced new logistics solutions to be used globally. As an international forum, the centre creates a space for exchanging information and discussing the latest developments," he says.

Mr. Nieszner said that DHL's focus on selected industry sectors means customers benefit from working with specialists—not just in logistics, but also in their particular marketplace.

"Our aim is to build long-term partnerships and work closely with our customers—often shoulder to shoulder with their management teams. The expertise of our people combined with our industry—leading solutions provides them with real competitive advantage. Our key industry sectors are life sciences and health care, technology and energy and the other sectors we are approaching are aerospace, automotive, consumer, fashion, engineering and manufacturing, mail order *B2C* and retail."

He emphasizes that corporate responsibility is a core element of the company's corporate strategy.

"Acting responsibly as a company means we treat our employees, the environment, the interests of society and the capital that has been entrusted to us in a manner that is respectful and ***sustainable***. Only in this way can we be successful in the long term," he says.

He explains that GoHelp is the company's global engagement in disaster management. Working closely with the United Nations Office for the Coordination of Humanitarian Affairs (OCHA) since 2005, a global network of Disaster Response Teams (DRTs) was created, made up of around 300 specially trained DHL employees.

"We provide the ideal global network for helping people impacted by major natural disasters and our support, ***in cooperation with*** the United Nations, focuses on global programs in two core areas: Immediate disaster response after natural disasters and disaster preparedness. "With the education program GoTeach, we support education and equality of access to education worldwide. As a large organization with high demand for qualified employees, we cannot afford to ignore the difficulties in education today and leave the responsibility to others. We are aware that our continued success as an organization is reliant upon well-educated employees across the whole range of educational qualification levels.

He points out that DHL is committed to minimizing the impact of its business on the environment. By 2020, the company aims to improve its CO_2 efficiency by 30%.

"Our core businesses, mail and logistics, result in emissions of carbon dioxide, making climate protection the primary focus of our efforts. However, our environmental protection program, GoGreen, also sets the stage for our environmental management system, covering the local management of aspects such as water, waste, noise, the use of natural resources and local air pollution.

"The primary objectives ***laid down*** in our environmental policy are as follows: to achieve transparency of our environmental impact, to improve operational efficiency, to generate value in offering green solutions to our customers as well as to foster green technologies, helping to shape political regulations and engaging with our key stakeholders. Further, we aim to mobilize employees in strengthening their environmental knowledge and helping them to engage in environmental protection." DHL also encourages and supports employees in their commitments towards volunteer projects. Introduced in Asia Pacific in 2008, Volunteer Day has expanded into the Americas, the

Middle East, Africa and Europe over the years, and continues to build on its success by involving more employees than ever before. Moreover, customers and business partners are also invited to be a part of the activities.

In each country, the DHL divisions individually choose projects for Global Volunteer Day to carry out. The projects include such activities as renovating school buildings in S. Africa, planting trees for reforestation in Serbia, transporting school supplies and donating blood.

New words and expressions

entrepreneurial	*adj.*	创业者的
expertise	*n.*	专门知识
forwarding	*n.*	运输业务
orientation	*n.*	方向；定向
overland	*adj.*	陆上的；经由陆路的
scenario	*n.*	设想
segment	*n.*	分出的或标出的一部分
sustainable	*adj.*	可持续的
tangible	*adj.*	切实的
unparalleled	*adj.*	无比的
B2C (Business to Customer)		企业对消费者的电子商务模式
in cooperation with		与……合作
lay down		制定；主张
umbrella brand		主品牌

Critical thinking

Work in groups and discuss the following questions.

(1) If you want to start a logistics company, what should you take into consideration?

(2) What should you do if your logistics company wants to be second-to-none?

(3) Supposing that your logistics company delay shipment, what should you do as a manager?

Unit 12

Staff Management

Staff management is the management of subordinates in an organization. Often, large organizations have many of these functions performed by a specialist department, such as Personnel or Human Resources (HR). The tasks of human resources include employment, training, retention, and other tasks to deal with employees inside an organization.

Learning objectives

* To define and use vocabulary of staff management;
* To conduct job analysis;
* To extract the main ideas from a listening text about job analysis;
* To compose a CV.

Warm-up questions

(1) Which activities do you think are related to staff management?

(2) Why is staff management important to a company?

Part A
General business vocabulary

1. **Match the words or phrases in the box with the following descriptions.**

A. layoff	B. CV	C. outsource	D. pension
E. job sharing	F. transfer	G. resign	H. flextime
I. bonus	J. recruit		

(1) This word means to find suitable people and get them to join a company, an organization, the armed forces, etc. It also refers to a person who has recently joined a company, organization, etc.

(2) It is an extra payment received by employees for doing their job well.

(3) This means the temporary suspension or permanent termination of employment of an employee or (more commonly) a group of employees for business reasons, such as when certain positions are no longer necessary or when a business slow-down occurs.

(4) It is an outline of a person's educational and professional history, usually prepared for job applications.

(5) It refers to moving employees either laterally or downward.

(6) It refers to allocating some noncore functions to outside specialists.

(7) It is a variable work schedule, in contrast to traditional work arrangements requiring employees to work a standard 9 am to 5 pm day.

(8) It is a fixed sum to be paid regularly to a person, typically following retirement from service.

(9) It refers to the situation in which two people divide the responsibility of one full-time job.

(10) This verb means to give up (a job or position) in a formal or official way.

2. Listen to the conversations and answer the questions.

(1) What job is the applicant applying for?

(2) Why does the applicant want a new job?

(3) Does the applicant have experience in accounting management?

(4) How are employees evaluated?

(5) What does the applicant need to apply for this job?

(6) Why doesn't the applicant get the job?

(7) How is the salary decided?

(8) Why did the applicant leave the first job?

Part B
Reading

Job Analysis

[1] A job analysis is a step-by-step **specification** of an employment position's requirements, functions, and procedures. Just as a seed cannot blossom into a flower unless the ground is properly prepared, many **human resource management** (HRM) practices cannot blossom into **competitive advantage** unless grounded on an adequate job analysis. Successful HRM practices can lead to outcomes that create competitive advantage. Job analyses, properly performed, **enhance** the success of these HRM practices by laying the foundation. Job analysis information can be applied to a variety of HRM practices.

[2] An employer's **recruitment** and selection practices seek to **identify** and hire the most suitable **applicants**. Job analysis information helps employers achieve this aim by identifying selection **criteria**, such as the knowledge, skills, and abilities (KSAs) needed to perform a job successfully. A firm's managers and human resource (HR) professionals can then use this information to choose or develop the appropriate selection devices (e.g., interview questions, tests). This approach to selection is legally required.

Establishing fair and effective hiring practices

[3] An employer facing discrimination **charges** must demonstrate to the courts that its selection criteria are job-related. To support this type of claim-relatedness, a firm must

demonstrate that the challenged selection practice was developed on the basis of job analysis information. As one judge noted during a discrimination *hearing*, without a job analysis on which to base selection practices, an employer "is aiming in the dark and can only hope to achieve job-relatedness by blind luck". In the 1990s, the need for firms to base selection criteria on job analysis information became even more important due to the passage of *the Americans with Disabilities Act*. This law states that employment decisions concerning disabled candidates must be based on their ability to perform the essential functions of the job. For instance, if report reading were an essential job function, then applicants whose disabilities prevented them from reading could be lawfully denied employment (assuming there was no way to *accommodate* them). If, however, report reading were not an essential function, the inability to read could not lawfully serve as a basis for *denial*. The determination of which job functions are essential is made during a job analysis.

Developing training and *appraisal* programs

[4] Firms can also use job analysis information to *assess* training needs and to develop and evaluate training programs. Job analysis can identify tasks a worker must perform. Then, through the performance appraisal process, supervisors can identify which tasks are being performed properly or improperly. The supervisor can next determine whether improperly performed work can be corrected through training.

[5] HR professionals also use job analysis information to develop relevant training programs. The job analysis *specifies* how each job is performed, step by step, allowing HR professionals to develop training materials to teach *trainees* how to perform each task. To evaluate the effectiveness of a training program, the organization must first specify training objectives or the level of performance expected of trainees when they finish the program. The success of a training program is judged on the basis of the extent to which those performance levels have been reached. Expected performance levels are often specified during a job analysis.

[6] Information obtained from job analysis can be used to develop performance appraisal forms. An example of a job analysis-based form would be one that lists the job's tasks or behaviors and specifies the expected performance level for each. The role of job analysis is crucial here. Without job analysis information, organizations typically use a single, generalized form in which all workers are appraised on the basis of a common set of characteristics or traits that are *presumed* to be needed for all jobs (e.g., cooperation, dependability, leadership).

[7] Job analysis-based appraisal forms are superior to the generalized forms because they

do a better job of communicating performance expectations and because they provide a better basis for giving feedback and for making HRM decisions.

New words and expressions

accommodate	[ə'kɒmədeɪt]	*vt.*	容纳，使适应
applicant	['æplɪknt]	*n.*	申请人，求职者
appraisal	[ə'preɪzl]	*n.*	评价，鉴定
assess	[ə'ses]	*vt.*	评估
charge	[tʃɑːdʒ]	*n.*	控告，指控
criteria	[kraɪ'tɪərɪə]	*n.*	标准，条件（单数：criterion）
denial	[dɪ'naɪl]	*n.*	拒绝
enhance	[ɪn'hɑːns]	*vt.*	提高，加强
hearing	['hɪərɪŋ]	*n.*	听证会，审讯
identify	[aɪ'dentɪfaɪ]	*vt.*	确定，识别，辨认出
presume	[prɪ'zjuːm]	*vt.*	假定；推测
recruitment	[rɪ'kruːtmənt]	*n.*	招聘
specification	[ˌspesɪfɪ'keɪʃn]	*n.*	说明，规范
specify	['spesɪfaɪ]	*vt.*	详细说明
trainee	[treɪ'niː]	*n.*	受训者，实习生
competitive advantage			竞争优势
human resource management			人力资源管理
job analysis			职务分析
the Americans with Disabilities Act			《美国残疾人法案》。该法案由美国国会在 1990 年 7 月通过，由老布什总统签署生效。2008 年小布什总统又签署了《残疾人法案修正案》，2009 年 1 月 1 日生效。它规定了残疾人所应享有的权利，特别是就业方面不应受到歧视。

Reading comprehension

1. **Work in pairs and decide whether the following statements are True (T) or False (F).**

   (1) A job analysis is merely relevant to the requirements of an employment position.

   (2) Successful HRM practices are based on a proper job analysis.

   (3) The appropriate selection criteria can help the boss to recruit the suitable applicants.

   (4) With a detailed job analysis, an employer can deny any disabled applicant.

(5) Job analyses can be used to identify tasks a worker must perform, and they can also help firms to assess training needs.

(6) Performance appraisals can only be conducted on the basis of job analysis.

2. Choose the best answer to fill in each blank.

(1) The sunshine will bring out the _____.
    A. blunder   **B.** blossom   **C.** block   **D.** blouse

(2) Good secretarial skills should _____ your chances of getting the job.
    A. enhance   **B.** enlarge   **C.** strengthen   **D.** magnify

(3) This rule cannot be _____ to every case.
    A. adopted   **B.** utilized   **C.** applied   **D.** employed

(4) Please _____ how the machine works.
    A. display   **B.** demonstrate   **C.** defense   **D.** indicate

(5) Success in making money is not always a good _____ of success in life.
    A. criterion   **B.** concept   **C.** condition   **D.** component

(6) The consequence of _____ is that people who have been discriminated will lose an equal opportunity.
    A. discrimination   **B.** disability   **C.** discount   **D.** disagreement

(7) He will never _____ anything if he doesn't work hard.
    A. reach   **B.** achieve   **C.** reap   **D.** arrive

(8) This house can _____ a family of five.
    A. accord   **B.** accrue   **C.** accordingly   **D.** accommodate

(9) We should _____ a time and a place for the meeting.
    A. except   **B.** species   **C.** specify   **D.** special

(10) I _____ you are here on business.
    A. resume   **B.** consume   **C.** prepare   **D.** presume

Part C
Listening

Listen to the conversation "How to Choose a Manager". Decide whether the following statements are True (T) or False (F).

(1) It is always easy to find good managers.

(2) An improvement in management can contribute more than any other factor to increase productivity.

(3) When one member of a group is promoted, there may be bad feeling among the others.

(4) People who are hired as skilled accountants or secretaries may not necessarily make good managers, and their personal development cannot be predicted.

(5) Low-level managers are generally judged by their achievements.

New words and expressions

accountant	[ə'kaʊntənt]	*n.*	会计师，会计人员
advance	[əd'vɑːns]	*n.*	发展，前进
advancement	[əd'vɑːnsmnt]	*n.*	前进，进步，提升
inducement	[ɪn'djuːsmənt]	*n.*	诱因，刺激物
intensify	[ɪn'tensɪfaɪ]	*vi.*	增强　*vt.* 使加强
overnight	[əʊvə'naɪt]	*adv.*	在夜间
physicist	['fɪzɪsɪst]	*n.*	物理学家
productivity	[prɒdʌk'tɪvətɪ]	*n.*	生产力，生产率，生产能力
subordinate	[sə'bɔːdɪnət]	*n.*	下属，下级，部属，属下
supervisor	['suːpəvaɪzə]	*n.*	主管
ultimately	['ʌltɪmətlɪ]	*adv.*	最后，根本，基本上
vacancy	['veɪkənsɪ]	*n.*	空缺，空位
competitive standing			竞争地位
from within			从里面，从……的内部
have the final say			有最终决定权，说了算
on account of			由于，因为，为了……的缘故

Part D
Translating

Translate the following sentences into English.

(1) 人力资源管理包括规划、雇用、维护、开发以及评估组织人力资源所涉及的全部活动。

(2) 在具体选择过程中，人力资源工作的要旨并非在于雇用最高素质的人选，而是要选择最适合于某一岗位的人来做那项工作，人尽其才。

(3) 求职者的受教育程度、工作经验、个人履历等方面的情况对于就业是非常重要的。

(4) 必须精心制定企业的酬金制度才能既满足员工们的需求，同时也把劳工成本控制在一个合理的范围内。

(5) 绩效评估评价职工目前和潜在的绩效水平，以便使管理者做出客观的人力资源决策。

Part E
Writing skills: CV

写作提示

CV 是个人简历（履历）的简称。和 resume 相比较，CV 通常更加详细，涵盖更加全面，也比 resume 更为严格。

当你申请工作时，特别是在科研教育、学术研究方面（如留学或申请奖学金），你需要提供 CV。在美国，CV 主要是用于申请学术、教育、科研职位，或者申请奖学金，等等，而在欧洲、非洲和亚洲等地，CV 则更常用于应聘工作。

Example

Jack Doe

90 WoodAvenue, Apartment #23

TeacherHill, MA 01832

978-212-64447

E-mail: jackdoe@yahoo.com

Career objective

A full-time position in ***Sales*** where I can demonstrate my technical and business skills and contribute to the company.

Summary of qualifications

• MBA	• Application Support	• Chemical Engineering
• Professional Engineer (P.E.)	• P&L Responsibility	• OEM Sales
• Product Marketing	• Contract Negotiations	• Account Management
• Project Management	• Quality Control	• Business Development
• Compound Semiconductor	• Wastewater Treatment	• Pre- and Post- Sales Support

Achievements

BOC Group Stock-Option Award for Outstanding Performance One of a dozen employees selected out of 45,000 employees worldwide to receive this award.	2002
Best Sales Specialist Award—BOC Edwards	1999
Professional Engineer (P.E.)	1997
Two Technical Publications	1996—1999
Fellowship and Research Assistantship Awards University of New Hampshire	1990—1992

Professional experience

• Managed all technical and commercial aspects of a five-year, $8 million, IBM 300mm contract.

• Developed sales tools and grew eastern region's sales from $1M in 1999 to $6M in 2003.

• Championed a new product-line (Zenith) for MOCVD application and sold the first six systems, $250K/system, in USA.

• Performed day-to-day product sales, marketing, and service activities.

• Provided technical and application support to Compound Semiconductor, MEMS, Automobile, Nano-technology and several high-tech industries.

• Identified and developed a new market for vacuum and abatement products—Compound Semiconductor.

• Supervised and managed quality assurance of $27M equipment decontamination at a superfund site.

Education

• **F. W. Olin Graduate School of Business at Babson College (Wellesley, MA)** Master of Business Administration (MBA) with concentration on marketing	2002
• **University of New Hampshire (Durham, NH)** Master of Science degree in Chemical Engineering	1992
• **Osmania University (Hyderabad, India)** Bachelor of Science degree in Chemical Engineering	1990

Employment history

• **BOC Edwards (Wilmington, MA)** Sales and Marketing Specialist	1996—1998
• **Nobis Engineering (Concord, NH)** Project Engineer	1994—1996
• **National Environmental Systems (Seekonk, MA)** Applications Engineer	1993—1994

References

Available upon request

Case writing

Task: You are applying for a job as a sales person in an insurance company. Write a CV including your personal information, education, work experience, and awards and honors if any.

Write in about **120-140** words.

Part F
Further business story

Human Resources Management

The human resource is not only unique and valuable; it is an organization's most important resources. The term "human resources" implies that people have capabilities that drive organizational performance (along with other resources such as money, materials, information, and the like). Other terms such as "human capital" and "intellectual assets" all have in common the idea that people make the difference in how an organization performs. It seems logical that organizations would *expend* a great deal of effort to acquire and *utilize* such a resource, and most organizations do. That effort is now known as human resource management, or HRM. It has also been called *staffing* and personnel management.

Human resources management consists of all the activities involved in planning, acquiring, maintaining, developing, and appraising an organization's human resources. As the definition implies, HRM begins with planning to ensure that personnel needs will be constantly and appropriately met. Then, acquisition—getting people to work for the organization. After this, steps must be taken to keep these valuable resources (they are the only business resources that can leave the organization at will). Next, the human resources should be developed to their full capacity to contribute to the firm. Finally, each employee's work should be measured against the performance standards or objectives established for his or her job.

In general, human resources management is a shared responsibility of line managers and staff HRM specialists. In very small organizations, the owner is usually both a line manager and the staff personnel *specialist*. He or she handles all or most HRM activities. As the firm grows in size, a personnel manager is generally hired to take over most of the staff responsibilities. As growth continues, additional staff positions are added as needed. In large firms, HRM activities tend to be very highly specialized. There may be separate groups to deal with *compensation*, training and development programs, and the other staff activities.

Human resources planning

Human resources planning is the development of strategies for meeting the firm's future human resource need. The starting point for this planning is the organization's overall strategic plan. From this, human resources planner can forecast the firm's future demand for human resources. Next they must determine whether the needed human resources will be available; that is, they must forecast the supply of human resources within the firm. Finally they have to take steps to match supply with demand.

Recruiting

Recruiting is the process of attracting qualified job applicants. Because it is a *vital* link in a costly process, recruiting needs to be a systematic rather than *haphazard* process. One goal of *recruiters* is to attract the "right" number of applicants. The right number is enough to allow a good match between applicants and open positions, but not so many that matching them requires too much time and effort.

Selection

Selection is the process of gathering information about applicants for a position and then using that information to choose the most appropriate applicant. Note the use of the word "appropriate". In selection, the idea is not to hire the person with the "most" qualifications, but rather to choose the applicant with the qualifications that are most appropriate for the job. The actual selection of an applicant often is made by one or more line managers who have responsibility for the position being filled. However, HRM personnel usually *facilitate* the selection process by developing *a pool of* applicants and *expediting* the *assessment* of the applicants. The most common means of obtaining information about applicants' qualifications are employment applications, tests, interview, references, and assessment center.

Employment applications are useful in collecting *factual* information on a candidate's education, work experience, and personal history. The data obtained from applications are usually used for two purposes: to identify candidates who are worthy of further *scrutiny* and to familiarize interviewers with applicants' backgrounds. Tests that are given to job candidates usually focus on *aptitudes*, skills, abilities, or knowledge relevant to the job that is to be performed. The employment interview, which provides an opportunity for the applicant and the firm to learn more about each other, is perhaps the most widely used selection technique.

Orientation

Soon after a candidate joins the firm, he or she goes through the firm's orientation program. Orientation is the process of *acquainting* new employees with the organization to help the selected individuals fit smoothly into the organization. Newcomers are introduced to their colleagues, acquainted with their responsibilities, and informed about the organization's culture, policies, and expectations regarding employee behavior.

Compensation

Attracting and hiring new employees is of vital importance. The firm's compensation system—the policies and strategies that determine employee compensation—must therefore be carefully designed to provide for employee needs while keeping *labor costs* within reasonable limits.

Training and development

Training and development are both aimed at improving employees' skills and abilities. Needless to say, new employees need training to do their jobs well. Experienced employees, in order to be more productive, also need training in more efficient techniques, methods or skills. A variety of methods are available for employee training and management development. They are on-the-job method, **vestibule training**, classroom teaching and lectures, conferences and *seminars* as well as role-playing.

Evaluation

Performance appraisal is the evaluation of employees' current and potential levels of performance to allow managers to make objective human resources decisions. The various techniques and methods for appraising employee performance are either objective or **judgmental** in nature. No matter which appraisal technique is used, the results should be discussed with the employee soon after the evaluation is completed. The information provided to an employee in such discussion is called **performance feedback**.

If a firm has done a good job in human resources management, the number of employees who fail to meet the firm's expectation will be very small. Most of the employees should be carefully selected, adequately trained, well developed, fairly compensated, and highly motivated. Such a workforce will be an **invaluable** asset to the organization, and contribute greatly to the business success and growth.

New words and expressions

acquaint	*vt.*	使熟悉；使认识
aptitude	*n.*	才能，能力
assessment	*n.*	评定；估价
compensation	*n.*	补偿；报酬
expedite	*vt.*	加快；促进
expend	*vt.*	花费；消耗
facilitate	*vt.*	促进；帮助
factual	*adj.*	事实的；真实的
haphazard	*adj.*	偶然的；随便的
invaluable	*adj.*	无价的；非常贵重的
judgmental	*adj.*	主观判断的
orientation	*n.*	情况介绍，雇员上岗指导
recruiter	*n.*	招聘人员
scrutiny	*n.*	详细审查
seminar	*n.*	讨论会，研讨班
specialist	*n.*	专家
staffing	*n.*	人员配置

utilize	vt.	利用
vital	adj.	至关重要的
a pool of		一群
labor cost		劳动力成本
performance feedback		绩效反馈
vestibule training		技工训练

Critical thinking

Work in groups and discuss the following questions.

(1) What should you have in mind if you are going to apply for a job in a company?

(2) What is the difference between human resource and other resources in a company?

(3) Why is HR management important?

Unit 13
Business Ethics

The field of ethics is a branch of philosophy that seeks virtue. Ethics deals with morality about what is considered "right" and "wrong" behavior for people in various situations. Business ethics is a form of applied ethics or professional ethics that examines ethical principles and moral or ethical problems that arise in a business environment.

Learning objectives

* To understand the definition and interpretation of business ethics;
* To distinguish the differences between business ethics and laws;
* To identify the main ideas and details from a listening idea;
* To learn to compose an application letter.

Warm-up questions

(1) Do you think that business ethics is important for the success of a company? Why or why not?

(2) What is business ethics?

Part A
General business vocabulary

1. Match the words in the box with the following descriptions.

A. governance	B. board	C. taxation	D. liability
E. espionage	F. entity	G. executive	H. takeover

(1) The purpose of the activity is to find out secret information and give it to a country's enemies or a company's competitors secretly.

(2) It is a legal responsibility for something, especially for paying money that is owed, or for damage or injury.

(3) A company is involved in the production, buying, and selling of goods or services for profit.

(4) This is an act of taking control of a company by buying most of its shares.

(5) It is a person or a group in a business organization, trade union who has administrative or managerial powers.

(6) It is about the act or process of controlling or directing the public affairs of a city, country, etc.

(7) A group of people in a company or other organization make the rules and important decisions.

(8) The aim of the system is to charge taxes.

2. Listen to the conversations and answer the questions.

(1) What are the two speakers talking about?

(2) What is the outcome of advertising for children today?

(3) What is the second speaker's attitude towards adverting promoting financial products on TV?

(4) What is the conversation about?

(5) What should the company do to solve the problem according to the first speaker?

(6) What is the reaction of the salesperson on the phone when hearing the complaint?

(7) What will the sale manager of the company do?

(8) Why does the man have the right to ask his company to pay for the fees?

Part B
Reading

Business Ethnics

[1] Business ethics (also corporate ethics) is a form of applied ethics or professional ethics that examines ethical principles and moral or ethical problems that arise in a business environment. It applies to all aspects of business conduct and is relevant to the conduct of individuals and entire organizations.

[2] Business ethics refers to contemporary standards or sets of values that govern the actions and behavior of an individual in the business organization.

[3] Business ethics has ***normative*** and descriptive dimensions. As a corporate practice and a career specialization, the field is primarily normative. Academics attempting to understand business behavior employ descriptive methods. The range and quantity of business ethical issues reflects the interaction of profit-maximizing behavior with non-economic concerns. Interest in business ethics ***accelerated*** dramatically during the 1980s and 1990s, both within major corporations and within ***academia***. For example, most major corporations today promote their commitment to non-economic values under headings such as ethics codes and social responsibility charters. Adam Smith said, "People of the same trade seldom meet together, even for ***merriment*** and ***diversion***, but the conversation ends in a conspiracy against the public, or in some ***contrivance*** to raise prices." Governments use laws and regulations to point business behavior in what they perceive to be beneficial directions. Ethics implicitly regulates areas and details of behavior that lie beyond governmental control. The emergence of large corporations with limited relationships and sensitivity to the communities in which they operate accelerated the development of formal ethics ***regimes***.

[4] Business ethics reflects the philosophy of business, of which one aim is to determine the fundamental purposes of a company. If a company's purpose is to maximize shareholder returns, then sacrificing profits to other concerns is a violation of its *fiduciary* responsibility. Corporate *entities* are legally considered as persons in USA and in most nations. The "corporate persons" are legally entitled to the rights and *liabilities* due to citizens as persons.

[5] Ethics are the rules or standards that govern our decisions on a daily basis. Many equate "ethics" with conscience or a simplistic sense of "right" and "wrong". Others would say that ethics is an internal code that governs an individual's conduct, *ingrained* into each person by family, faith, tradition, community, laws, and personal mores. Corporations and professional organizations, particularly licensing boards, generally will have a written "Code of Ethics" that governs standards of professional conduct expected of all in the field. It is important to note that "law" and "ethics" are not synonymous, nor are the "legal" and "ethical" courses of action in a given situation necessarily the same. Statutes and regulations passed by legislative bodies and administrative boards set forth the "law". Slavery once was legal in the US, but one certainly wouldn't say enslaving another was an "ethical" act.

[6] Economist Milton Friedman writes that corporate executives' "responsibility... generally will be to make as much money as possible while conforming to their basic rules of the society, both those embodied in law and those embodied in ethical custom". Friedman also said, "the only entities who can have responsibilities are individuals... A business cannot have responsibilities. So the question is, do corporate executives, provided they stay within the law, have responsibilities in their business activities other than to make as much money for their stockholders as possible? And my answer to that is, no, they do not." A multi-country 2011 survey found support for this view among the "informed public" ranging from 30% to 80%. Ronald Duska views Friedman's argument as *consequentialist* rather than *pragmatic*, implying that unrestrained corporate freedom would benefit the most in long term. Similarly author business consultant Peter Drucker observed, "There is neither a separate ethics of business nor is one needed," implying that standards of personal ethics cover all business situations. However, Peter Drucker in another instance observed that the ultimate responsibility of company directors is not to harm. Another view of business is that it must exhibit Corporate Social Responsibility (CSR): an *umbrella term* indicating that an ethical business must act as a responsible citizen of the communities in which it operates even at the cost of profits or other goals. In the US and most other nations corporate entities are legally treated as persons in some respects. For example, they can hold title to property, *sue* and be sued and are subject to *taxation*, although their free speech rights are limited. This can be interpreted to imply that

they have independent ethical responsibilities. Duska argues that stakeholders have the right to expect a business to be ethical; if business has no ethical obligations, other institutions could make the same claim which would be *counterproductive* to the corporation.

[7] Ethical issues include the rights and duties between a company and its employees, suppliers, customers and neighbors, its fiduciary responsibility to its shareholders. Issues concerning relations between different companies include *hostile take-overs* and industrial *espionage*. Related issues include corporate *governance*, corporate social *entrepreneurship*, political contributions, legal issues such as the ethical debate over introducing a crime of corporate manslaughter, and the marketing of corporations' ethics policies. According to *IBE* research published in late 2012, the three major areas of public concern regarding business ethics in Britain are executive pay, corporate tax avoidance and bribery and corruption.

New words and expressions

academia	[ˌækə'diːmɪə]	*n.*	学术界
accelerate	[ək'seləreɪt]	*vt.*	使……增速
consequentialist	[ˌkɒnsə'kwenʃəlɪst]	*n.*	结果论者
contrivance	[kən'traɪvns]	*n.*	计谋
counterproductive	[ˌkaʊntəprə'dʌktɪv]	*adj.*	事与愿违；适得其反
diversion	[daɪ'vɜːʃn]	*n.*	消遣
entity	['entətɪ]	*n.*	实体
entrepreneurship	[ˌɒntrəprə'nɜːʃɪp]	*n.*	企业家精神
espionage	['espɪənɑːʒ]	*n.*	间谍活动
fiduciary	[fɪ'djuːʃ(ə)rɪ]	*adj.*	信托的
governance	['gʌvənəns]	*n.*	管理
ingrain	[ɪn'greɪn]	*vt.*	使……根深蒂固
liability	[laɪə'bɪlətɪ]	*n.*	责任
merriment	['merɪmnt]	*n.*	欢喜
normative	['nɔːmətɪv]	*adj.*	规范的
pragmatic	[præg'mætɪk]	*adj.*	实用主义的
regime	[reɪ'ʒiːm]	*n.*	管理体制
sue	[sjuː]	*vt.*	控告；请求
taxation	[tæk'seɪʃn]	*n.*	征税；税款
hostile take-over			敌意收购
IBE (The Institute of Business Ethics)			商业道德研究所。总部设在伦敦的非营利性专业组织。它倡导以伦理价值为基础的高标准商业行为。该组织旨在提高公众在经商时遵守伦理道德的重要性意

识的同时与英国或国际上的其他组织在
利益和商业伦理专长方面展开合作。

umbrella term   涵盖性术语

Reading comprehension

1. Work in pairs and discuss the following questions according to the passage.

(1) What does business ethics refer to?

(2) What are the two dimensions of business ethics?

(3) How do you understand the statement given by Adam Smith?

(4) Why can't ethics be simply interpreted as "law"?

(5) Why are corporate entities in the US and most other nations regarded as persons in some aspects?

2. Choose the best answers to explain the meanings of the underlined words.

(1) The EU wants such a treaty to prevent the <u>diversion</u> of conventional weapons to the illicit market and to include transparency, monitoring and assistance provisions.

    A. version   **B.** conclusion   **C.** deviation   **D.** mission

(2) The following <u>normative</u> documents contain provision which, through reference in this text, constitute provisions of this national standard.

    A. prescriptive   **B.** active   **C.** imaginative   **D.** initiative

(3) GDP was called one of the greatest <u>contrivance</u> in 20th century which is a popular macroeconomic calculating index in worldwide countries.

    A. surveillance   **B.** devisal   **C.** conveyance   **D.** controversy

(4) This license is the least restrictive of all Microsoft licenses and essentially says you can do whatever you want as long as you keep the copyright notices and do not <u>sue</u> the authors.

    A. value   **B.** pursue   **C.** summarize   **D.** prosecute

(5) Improved safety measures in cars can be <u>counterproductive</u> as they encourage people to drive faster.

    A. beneficial   **B.** attractive   **C.** respective   **D.** harmful

(6) They do not necessarily want to overthrow their <u>regime</u>, but to express the depths of their frustration with its inadequacy.

    A. government   **B.** organism   **C.** dimension   **D.** dime

(7) The goal is to <u>accelerate</u> the development of a monitoring solution for these industry verticals.

    A. exaggerate   **B.** decorate   **C.** hasten   **D.** liberate

(8) What really drives scientists to the far ends of the earth in search of new species is something far less <u>pragmatic</u>.

    A. critic   **B.** practical   **C.** characteristic   **D.** enthusiastic

(9) Nietzsche acknowledges that his inquiries into indebtedness and contractual <u>obligation</u> have so far ignored the moralization of these concepts.

    A. situation   **B.** responsibility   **C.** distribution   **D.** information

(10) Coaching can encourage you to <u>exhibit</u> the right body language, ingratiate yourself with the interviewer and better communicate your skills and experience.

    A. liberate   **B.** profit   **C.** permit   **D.** display

Part C
Listening

Listen to the conversation "Takata Air Bag Recall". Decide whether the following statements are True (T) or False (F).

(1) The Takata Corporation decides to recall millions of vehicles and replace millions of air bag inflators, because of the safety problems of these inflators.

(2) Customers can only give the Takata Corporate a call to know whether their cars have been recalled or not.

(3) The VIN check page will be updated as automakers announce more recalls.

(4) People can just wait about several months for the replacement of their inflators.

(5) Because of the lapses of Takata Corporation, all customers choose not to trust the company any more.

New words and expressions

ammonium	[ə'məunɪəm]	*n.*	铵
dash	[dæʃ]	*n.*	冲撞
degrade	[dɪ'ɡreɪd]	*vt.*	使……降解
deployment	[di:'plɔɪmənt]	*n.*	调度，部署
desiccant	['desɪknt]	*n.*	干燥剂
humidity	[hju:'mɪdətɪ]	*n.*	湿度；湿气
ignite	[ɪɡ'naɪt]	*v.*	点燃；使燃烧

inflator	[ɪn'fletə]	n.	增压泵
jamb	[dʒæm]	n.	门窗侧壁
lapse	[læps]	n.	判断错误
nitrate	['naɪtreɪt]	n.	硝酸盐
recur	[rɪ'kɜː]	vi.	复发；重现
rupture	['rʌptʃə]	n.	破裂
scroll	[skrəʊl]	vt.	（指计算机荧屏上的文本）逐渐上下移动
shrapnel	['ʃræpnl]	n.	榴霰弹
spew	[spjuː]	v.	喷出
vault	[vɔːlt]	n.	地下室

NHTSA (National Highway Traffic Safety Administration) 国家公路交通安全管理局
VIN (Vehicle Identification Number) 车辆识别号码

Part D
Translating

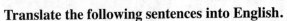

Translate the following sentences into English.

(1) 通常商业道德源于政治和文化环境背景下的个人道德标准。

(2) 公司邀请名人代言品牌时要慎重，因为名人的不当行为会损害品牌声誉。

(3) 企业发布可持续发展报告是现在的标准做法，但有些企业还是能找到方法秘密进行非法活动，如金融违规行为。

(4) 学者一般采用描述性方法以试图理解公司商业行为。

(5) 界定道德标准的两个最大挑战是：应该建立在什么样的标准之上，以及我们应该在特定情形下如何运用这些标准。

Part E
Writing skills: Application letter

写作提示

申请信（Application letter）有很多种，如求职信、就业申请信、调动工作申请信、辞职申请信、国外大学申请信等。

人们在求职时一般都需要写求职申请信。它的格式与普通书信一样，一般有信头、地址、称呼、正文、结尾（敬语）、签名等。

求职信需要注意几点：第一，一定要将自己的详细地址、电话号码写在日期上方，以便对方与写信人联系。第二，申请信的称呼要得当，写给认识或不认识、知道名字或不知道名字的称呼不相同。第三，申请信主体部分常分为开场白、正文和结尾三部分。第四，申请信一定要简单明了，不用客套话，开门见山，写清写信原因、兴趣等。第五，求职信的正文一定强调自己的学历和工作经历，如申请其他事项，应着重理由。第六，应在求职信的结尾表示希望参加面试，结尾敬语之前常加上 *"I would appreciate your early reply."* 之类的话。

求职信的结构（**Layout**）：

1. 信头（**Heading**）。写信人的单位名称、地址、电话、传真、邮编以及写信日期。信头的目的是使收信人一看便知求职信来自何处，何时写成，便于招聘单位回信。

2. 信内地址（**Inside address**）。收信人的姓名、地址、职位必须准确、具体。一般写在信头下面空一两行处，顶格写。

1）写给某个单位的个人，如：

Mr. Allen Smith

Yun Qing Oil Company

207 Huai Hai Road

Shanghai 200000

2）写给某单位不知名的负责人，如：

The Manager

Uni'Tech Electronics Corporation

216 Dahua Road

Jinjiang, Guangdong 519000

3）写给某个单位的人事部门，如：

Personnel Department

Shumei Textiles Industries

6 Nanchang Street

Wuxi, Jiangsu 214000

3. 称呼（**Salutation**）

不相识的男士 / 女士

Dear Sir/ Sirs, Gentlemen

Dear Madam

相识的男士 / 女士

Dear Mr. Sun/Mrs. Shen/Miss Gao

不知道收信人的姓名，用 *"To Whom It May Concern"*

4. 正文（**Body**）

5. 结尾客套语（**Complimentary close**）

6. 签名（**Signature**）

如果是打印的求职信，一定要在结束语和打印好的姓名之间空出两、三行，亲笔署名。

7. 附件（**Enclosure**）

求职者一般需随函附寄个人资料，这些资料统称为附件，顶格写在署名下的间隔一行处。若是英文求职信，两件以上用 *Enclosures* 表示，缩写为 *Encls.*

Example

Saint Michael's College

Burlington, Vermont 05439

April 9, 2020

Nicholas Slick

Ace Communications

100 Fifth Ave. New York, New York 10011

Dear Mr. Slick,

I'm writing to inquire about career opportunities in the fields of marketing and advertising. I am very interested in working Ace Advertising, especially in the Art Department.

I will be graduating from Saint Michael's College in May with a double major in Business Administration and Fine Arts. At Saint Michael's, I have developed a very unique educational experience that has combined the financial, theoretical, and practical aspects of a business education with the creativity and design theories of a fine arts education. I have also become proficient with the computer applications prevalent in these fields, particularly Adobe Photo Shop, and QuarkXPress. As an intern at XYZ Communications, a major advertising firm in Burlington, Vermont, I was part of a creative team responsible for developing the graphic images illustrating the advertising copy for magazine and billboard promotions. During the summer of 2017, I studied in Venezuela where I acquired insight into the business and artistic forces affecting marketing and advertising, especially in a global marketplace. As a result of these experiences, I am confident that I will bring both technical skills and a fresh perspective to the creative team at Ace Communications.

I am enclosing my resume. Samples of my work can be viewed online at www. onlineshow.com/studentresourcecenter. References are available upon request from the Student Resource Center at Saint Michael's College at (802) 654-25**.

I would appreciate an interview with you at your convenience. I will be available at my campus address until my graduation on May 13. After that I can be reached at my permanent address.

I would appreciate your early reply. Thank you for your consideration.

Sincerely yours,

Arthur Pallet

Enclosure: Resume

Case writing

Task: Write an Application Letter for a Position of Chief Information Officer to someone in Personnel Department of South Securities Agency. The address of the company is Shui-yin Road, Guangzhou and its Postcode is 5105×××. The following information should be included:

* your source of the information for the position;
* your personal information and your qualification;
* your contact information;
* your name is Bai Zhihua.

Write in about **150** words.

Part F
Further business story

The Enron Scandal and Ethics

Few names in American business are so *synonymous* with scandal and corruption as that of Enron. Even those who don't understand the basics of the story know one thing— Enron means bad business. Today, Enron is a case study in ethics and the story of one of the biggest *frauds* in American history.

An Enron Scandal introduction

At its simplest, the Enron scandal is about fraud, the complexities of *deregulation* and a system that rewards companies for how they look on paper. Of course, it goes far deeper than that, because it's also a story about how millions of people lost their savings by buying stock in a company that many deemed was too big to fail. It's also about how the watchers at the gate, including accounting firms like Arthur Andersen, can be *willfully complicit* in turning the other cheek to inflated numbers on balance books, because greed is a mighty motivator.

At its height, Enron was America's seventh largest company. Even now, people struggle to understand what Enron really did, since they didn't have a straight product to sell, like, say, Apple. Enron essentially created the way energy is traded on public markets. There was no framework for this before Enron engineered one. What happened next was their *hubris* got in the way, because if they could trade something so *intangible* as energy, why not trade everything?

Turns out that wasn't such a great plan, because failures began mounting. That's where Jeff Skilling's accounting *wiles* came to the creative rescue—Enron invented partner companies through which they could *offset* or hide their losses, leaving the stock market's darling looking great on paper. But, after a *meteoric* rise from Enron's *inception* in 1985, the year 2001 finally brought *scrutiny* and skepticism. With the SEC and others poking holes in the veil of Enron's lies, soon the whole *facade* was exposed and a *cautionary* tale for the ages was *writ*.

What caused the Enron Scandal?

In the 1980s, Wall Street rejoiced as deregulation (especially surrounding energy) meant markets opened and became freer. This allowed for all kinds of new, innovative trading for those who saw the potential. By the 1990s, the "dot-com bubble" was growing wildly with share values commonly being padded to wow and woo investors.

If a company looked solid on paper, it performed well in the market, which was where Enron got its juice. It was CEO Jeff Skilling who decided to change Enron's accounting approach from the traditional historical cost accounting method to the mark-to-market (MTM) method, and this changed everything, helping the company to reach its *stratospheric* heights of over $90 a share in August 2000 (and which would plunge to $0.26 a share by December 2001).

MTM accounting is legitimately used by many companies on a regular basis, but it's easily misused by those looking for something to hide, like Enron. As Investopedia explains, "The method can be manipulated, since MTM is not based on 'actual' cost but on 'fair value', which is harder to pin down. Some believe MTM was the beginning of the end for Enron as it essentially permitted the organization to log estimated profits as actual profits." Basically, this method meant Enron could count projected long-term energy contract earnings as current income, thus cooking their books, which was one of the key Enron ethical issues.

Fallout from Enron

When all was done and dusted, the estimated losses from the Enron scandal clocked in around $74 billion. Around 4,500 people lost their jobs, many receiving little in their settlements, most capping out to a max of $13,500.

Execs, however, scandalously cleaned out the *coffers* in 2000, paying themselves bonuses as the company's collapse *loomed*, leaving little to nothing for tens of thousands of investors who lost billions.

Did any Enron executives go to jail?

Several executives faced and were convicted of charges of *wire fraud* and *securities fraud* in the Enron scandal. The biggest names were Kenneth Lay, Jeffrey Skilling and Andrew Fastow.

Kenneth Lay: In 1985, Enron was formed as a result of a merger between Houston Natural Gas Company and Omaha-based InterNorth Incorporated. Kenneth Lay transitioned from being the CEO of HNG to leading Enron. Lay was convicted for his role in engineering the massive fraud but died of a heart attack before sentencing.

Jeffrey Skilling: CEO of subsidiary Enron Finance, Jeff Skilling abruptly resigned in August 2001, just as the cracks began to show in the parent company's *brazen* schemes. He was arrested in 2004 and sentenced to 28 years in prison. In 2013, a series of negotiations led to his term being reduced to 14 years. He was released in February 2019 and began making immediate waves as reports emerged of the 65-year-old ex-con's efforts to try to return to the energy sector.

Andrew Fastow: After cooperating with authorities and providing evidence, former CFO Fastow was found guilty and sentenced to five years in prison in 2006. He was released in 2011.

Enron Scandal: Ethics and consequences

Some may look at the jail time served by some Enron leaders as being the consequence of that scandal, but others lost their retirement savings and saw their entire lives transformed because they believed news headlines about Enron being America's "most innovative company" and bought shares. Tens of billions of dollars were lost, lives altered, investor confidence shaken and laws changed, all because a few executives let their egos get in the room when doing the accounting. The question that comes up, even now, is to whom is a company responsible? The public, the investors, the employees, themselves?

Whatever the answer, eventually Enron failed them all. It often comes down to the premise that just because something is legal doesn't mean it's ethical. Sure, the MTM accounting method is used in responsible, pragmatic ways daily, by all kinds of ethical companies, but it was also used by the likes of Enron to dupe millions of investors out of their life savings. As that happened, the seeming on-paper successes allowed Enron's execs to pay themselves ludicrous bonuses even as the end was drawing near. Kenneth Lay alone cashed in on over $152 million in bonuses in 2000, just as the farce was beginning its end.

The complexities of what was legal versus ethical is why Enron will remain a lesson in business classes for decades to come. And the scandal opened the door to new, critical laws, as Encyclopedia Britannica explains, "The most important of those measures, the Sarbanes-Oxley Act (2002), imposed harsh penalties for destroying, altering, or fabricating financial records. The act also prohibited auditing firms from doing any concurrent consulting business for the same clients."

New words and expressions

brazen	*adj.*	厚颜无耻的；无所顾忌的
cautionary	*adj.*	警告的，告诫的
coffer	*n.*	金库
complicit	*adj.*	有同谋关系的，串通一气的
deregulation	*n*	放松管制、解除管制
facade	*n.*	假象，伪装
fraud	*n.*	欺诈行为
hubris	*n.*	傲慢；狂妄自大
inception	*n.*	（机构、组织等的）开端，创始
intangible	*adj.*	不可捉摸的，难以确定的；（资产，利益）无形的
loom	*v.*	隐约可见
meteoric	*adj.*	大气的；流星的；疾速的
offset	*v.*	补偿，抵销；
scrutiny	*n.*	仔细审查
stratospheric	*adj.*	平流层的；同温层的
synonymous	*adj.*	同义的
wiles	*n.*	诡计，花招，花言巧语
willfully	*adv.*	任意地
writ	*n.*	[法] 令状；文书；法院命令
securities fraud		证券欺诈
wire fraud		电信欺诈

Critical thinking

Work in groups and discuss the following questions.

(1) Why do you choose to follow business ethics when you do business with others?

(2) If you figure out the drawbacks of your company's product, would you like to recall it? Why or why not?

(3) If your company recalls a certain kind of product, what would you to maintain the fame of your company?

Unit 14
Going Global

Globalization has transformed the way the world of business operates. Engaging in global commerce has increasingly become a non-negotiable aspect of business, particularly in developed markets where big challenges around economic growth are resulting in reduced opportunities at home. However, going global is no small feat for both small and large businesses alike, who face many challenges as they seek to gain traction abroad. Even tech startups, who are often much better funded when they expand into new markets, often struggle to grow internationally. Understanding the culture you're expanding your business to and forging the relationships you'll need to understand this culture should be the top of the list for every entrepreneur with international ambitions.

Learning objectives

* To list and define the vocabulary of globalization and cross-culture communication;
* To discuss the benefits of globalization;
* To spot details while listening;
* To demonstrate the skills of preparing for presentations.

Warm-up questions

(1) How do you understand globalization?

(2) List some barriers of cross-cultural communication and give the solutions to them.

Part A
General business vocabulary

1. **Match the words or phrases in the box with the following descriptions.**

> A. Multinational Corporation/Enterprise (MNC/MNE)
> B. World Bank   C. joint venture   D. economic integration
> E. International Monetary Fund (IMF)   F. World Trade Organization (WTO)
> G. sovereign state   H. multi-domestic   I. subsidiary
> J. economies of scale

(1) They are the cost advantages that enterprises obtain due to size, output, or scale of operation, with cost per unit of output generally decreasing with increasing scale as fixed costs are spread out over more units of output.

(2) It is an intergovernmental organization which regulates international trade.

(3) The company that has facilities and other assets in at least one country other than its home country.

(4) It is an international organization headquartered in Washington, D.C., of 189 countries working to foster global monetary cooperation, secure financial stability, facilitate international trade, promote high employment and sustainable economic growth, and reduce poverty around the world.

(5) It is an international financial institution that provides loans to developing countries for capital programs.

(6) It is the unification of economic policies between different states through the partial or full abolition of tariff and non-tariff restrictions on trade taking place among them.

(7) A strategy by which companies try to achieve maximum local responsiveness by customizing both their product offering and marketing strategy to match different national conditions.

(8) It is, in international law, a nonphysical juridical entity that is represented by one centralised government that has sovereignty over a geographic area.

(9) It is a business entity created by two or more parties, generally characterized by shared ownership, shared returns and risks, and shared governance.

(10) It is a company that is owned or controlled by another company, which is called the parent company, parent, or holding company.

2. Listen to the conversations and answer the questions.

(1) What can you learn about the role of American business behavior?

(2) What should we do if the company wants to be competent globally?

(3) What should be included in the training program?

(4) What topics have been mentioned here as the taboos of small talk in western culture?

(5) What does the speaker suggest to get professional advices?

(6) What kind of impression do Americans give on foreign negotiators?

(7) What are the traits that mainly cause cross-cultural misunderstanding on the part of American negotiators?

Part B
Reading

Multinational Corporations

[1] The term "economic globalization" is now being used with increasing frequency in newspapers, magazines, *seminars* and international conferences. With the basic feature of free flow of commodity, capital, technology, service, and information in the global context for *optimized allocation*, economic globalization is giving new *impetus* and providing opportunities to world economic development and meanwhile making the various economies more and more *interdependent* and interactive. Economy is not the only element involved in globalization since it also has an important *bearing* on politics, culture, value and way of life. While many people are *acclaiming* the benefits brought by economic globalization, there are also loud voices of opposition, since different countries and people do not enjoy balanced benefits. Economic integration

enables countries benefit from the boom of other countries but also makes them more *vulnerable* to the *adverse* events across the globe. Maybe we can say few topics are as *controversial* as globalization. But like it or not, it has become an objective trend in world economic development. The best policy for us is to follow the trend closely, *availing* the opportunities it offers to develop ourselves and avoiding its possible impacts.

[2] Such world organizations as WTO, World Bank and the International Monetary Fund which we shall discuss in this lesson, are, in a sense, champions of economic globalization, while the multinational corporations are directly engaged in the trend and their operations *constitute* the major content of economic globalization. Some knowledge of the multinationals will help us gain a better understanding of the global trend.

[3] Before World War II there were already a number of companies that would be described as multinationals. They were, however, *comparatively* small in number and scale. The first step in the internationalization of business after the War was simply a very rapid growth in fairly traditional terms, in the sense that more and more companies in one developed country set up their own, or bought over existing, manufacturing facilities in other countries.

[4] As development of such business activities grew rapidly, they had not only been variously defined in different studies, but also labeled with different names. However a typical multinational enterprise shall be defined as a business organization which owns, controls and manages assets, often including productive resources, in more than one country, through its member companies incorporated separately in each of these countries. Each member company is known as a multinational corporation. Each MNC is *purported* to represent certain interests of the multinational enterprise and is linked to one another within the organizational framework of the same multinational enterprise. If the MNC is the original investing corporation, it is known as the parent MNC, which normally also the international headquarters of the MNE. If the MNC is established as a result of investments by the MNE, whether through the parent or through another of its already established MNC, it is an *affiliate* MNC. An MNE may also have various regional or operational headquarters, in addition to its international headquarters.

[5] The multinationals have the following distinctive characteristics. Firstly, MNEs are generally enormous in size. For instance, General Electrics established in 1892 now has *subsidiaries* in over 100 countries and regions with more than 300,000 employees. Wide geographical spread is also characteristic of MNEs. Such geographical spread of MNEs enables them to have a wide range of options in terms of decisions in areas such as sourcing and pricing. They are also more able to take advantage of changes in the international economic environment. Such multinationality also enables MNEs to engage in worldwide integrated production and marketing giving rise to extensive intra-MNE

transactions which constitute a very significant proportion of total international trade. Another general characteristic of large MNEs is their longevity and rapid growth. Some MNEs have histories of many years and their double digit growth rate of revenue adjusted for inflation is higher than that of the GDP of many countries.

[6] The behavior of MNEs is very much determined by their needs. These needs are often identified as goals. The purpose of organization is to facilitate the MNEs' operations and the purpose of its operations is to achieve its organizational goals.

[7] Like most business organizations, MNEs are formed for profit. There is little doubt that the profit goal represents the basic need of the MNEs' shareholders. It is also the need of all groups interested in the continued survival of the MNE. Yet this interest in the continued survival of the MNE expresses a second basic need—that of security. The importance of security to the MNE cannot be doubted. Profit is useless if it cannot be secured by the MNE and transferred wherever it desires. Its assets and investments must be secured. A favorable business environment must also be secured.

[8] Multinational Corporations can be classified into four different types according to their organization and way of operation. The first type is called ***multi-domestic corporation***, which is a group of relatively independent subsidiaries. The parent company delegates sufficient power to each subsidiary to manage the production and marketing in the host country for the needs of local customers. The second type is the global corporations which operates under an opposite principle from the fist type and views the world market as an integrated whole. Power and responsibility are concentrated at the headquarters that manages production and marketing to achieve the economies of scale as much as possible. The third, the transnational corporation, aims to combine the advantages of the above two ways of operation so as to achieve both efficiency and flexibility. The activities and resources of the transnational corporation are neither highly centralized as the second type nor ***decentralized*** as the first type but are integrated in an interdependent network of affiliates. The fourth type can be referred to as world companies as their national identities are blurred to a large extent. Very few companies, if any, have reached this level of internationalization. But it is interesting to imagine the situation on the globe with the increase and growth of world companies. When such companies become dominating, the possibility of conflicts among ***sovereign states*** may be greatly reduced. Possibly they will be instrumental to the realization of complete globalization.

New words and expressions

acclaim	[ə'kleɪm]	*vt.*	称赞
adverse	['ædvɜːs]	*adj.*	不利的；相反的；敌对的
affiliate	[ə'fɪlɪeɪt]	*n.*	隶属的机构　*vt.* 使附属

allocation	[ˌæləˈkeɪʃn]	*n.*	分配，配置
avail	[əˈveɪl]	*vt.*	有益于，有益于
bearing	[ˈbeərɪŋ]	*n.*	关系
comparatively	[kəmˈpærətɪvlɪ]	*adv.*	相对地
constitute	[ˈkɒnstɪtjuːt]	*vt.*	组成，构成
controversial	[ˌkɒntrəˈvɜːʃl]	*adj.*	有争议的；有争论的
decentralized	[diˈsentrəlaɪzd]	*adj.*	分散的
impetus	[ˈɪmpɪtəs]	*n.*	动力
interdependent	[ˌɪntədɪˈpendənt]	*adj.*	相互依赖的
optimized	[ˈɒptɪmaɪzd]	*adj.*	最佳化的
purport	[pəˈpɔːt]	*vt.*	声称
seminar	[ˈsemɪnɑː]	*n.*	研讨会
subsidiary	[səbˈsɪdɪərɪ]	*adj.*	附属的；辅助的　*n.* 子公司
vulnerable	[ˈvʌlnərəbl]	*adj.*	易受攻击的，易受……的攻击
multi-domestic corporation			多国化公司
sovereign states			主权国家

Reading comprehension

1. Work in pairs and discuss whether the following statements are True (T) or False (F).

(1) All people speak highly of the benefits brought by economic globalization.

(2) There were already a large number of multinationals before World War II.

(3) MNE is the abbreviation for multinational enterprise.

(4) The MNC that is the original investing corporation is known as the international headquarters of the MNE.

(5) The two basic needs of MNE are profits and security.

2. Choose the best answers to explain the meanings of the underlined words.

(1) They have also provided most of the <u>stimulus</u> for the adoption of these practices.
    A. impromptu   **B.** impetus   **C.** prompt   **D.** importance

(2) The restaurant has been widely <u>praised</u> for its excellent French cuisine.
    A. claimed   **B.** declared   **C.** blamed   **D.** acclaimed

(3) Old people are particularly <u>unprotected</u> members of our society.
    A. volatile   **B.** voluble   **C.** vulnerable   **D.** voluntary

(4) He ignored all kinds of <u>unfavorable</u> comments about him.
    A. admiring   **B.** admissible   **C.** adverse   **D.** advisory

(5) China's ethnic minorities <u>make up</u> less than 7% of its total population.

    A. compound   **B.** consist   **C.** compose   **D.** constitute

(6) Documents leaked to this newspaper <u>claim</u> to reveal the radioactive waste is being illegally dumped on the site.

    A. puncture   **B.** purport   **C.** purge   **D.** pursue

(7) For example, consider the profit generated by a German <u>affiliate</u> of a French company.

    A. subsidiary   **B.** submissive   **C.** subordinate   **D.** subjective

(8) The European Parliament has voted for sweeping reforms of the <u>disputable</u> EU Common Fisheries Policy.

    A. contributive   **B.** controversial   **C.** conservative   **D.** converse

(9) Mandatory disclosure is an intrusion on the free market, but a <u>relatively</u> benign one.

    A. completely   **B.** competitively   **C.** compatibly   **D.** comparatively

(10) <u>Supreme</u> power will continue to lie with the Supreme People's Assembly.

    A. Solitary   **B.** Sophisticated   **C.** Sovereign   **D.** Solid

Part C
Listening

Listen to the conversation "The Strategy of Entering International Market". Decide whether the following statements are True (T) or False (F).

(1) Licensing is a double-edged sword as an effective way for a company to enter a foreign market.

(2) The advantage of joint venture is that we can avoid the possible conflicts among partners

(3) The best way to enter the foreign markets is to set up subsidiaries even though it demands a large investment.

(4) Since there is a strong demand of the product in the target market, there is no need for adaptation.

(5) All the suggestions delivered in the conversation are based on a full marketing research.

New words and expressions

adaptation	[ædæp'teɪʃn]	*n.*	适应
conflict	['kɒnflɪkt]	*n.*	冲突
		vi.	冲突

expire	[ɪkˈspaɪə]	*vi.*	期满
licensing	[ˈlaɪsnsɪŋ]	*n.*	许可
minimum	[ˈmɪnɪməm]	*n.*	最小值
payoff	[ˈpeɪɔːf]	*n.*	收益
terminate	[ˈtɜːmɪneɪt]	*vt.*	使终止
cater to			迎合
economy of scale			规模经济
give away			放弃，泄露，分发
result in			导致，结果是
to make matters worse			更糟的是

Part D
Translating

Translate the following sentences into English.

(1) 商业上的成功有赖于不同文化间的交流和有效的跨文化沟通技巧。

(2) 跨国公司可以利用不同国家的税收差异，在税率较低的国家开展业务。

(3) 一个失误或是误解都可能使几个月的工作成绩毁于一旦。

(4) 理解并意识到不同文化间的区别能促进更顺畅的沟通，有助于贸易双方破除障碍，建立信任，加强关系，打开商机。

(5) 显然，价值观的认知与差异会影响谈判结果。

Part E
Writing skills: Presentation

写作提示

　　报告（Presentation）是比较常见的，开会时经常有此项内容。Presentation 一般都采用多媒体辅助手段，设置投影仪，多用 PowerPoint 软件做演示。其表达方式非常丰富，有文字、表格、图形、图像、动画、声音等，能充分调动起听众的兴趣。

　　如何设计好的报告呢？与书面报告一样，一般来说，presentation 也分为三个部分：开篇介绍（Introduction），正文（Body），和总结部分（Closing or Conclusion）。开篇介绍要有吸引力，可以引用一些名言警句，讲幽默故事，还可以列举具体数据或提出一些引发思考的问题。然后，提出自己的关键主张。在正文部分，对观点的阐述一定要逻辑清楚，尽量将要点控制在三个以内。较长的报告阐述过程中，要注意适时总结前文观点，并对下文即将提出的观点进行预告。转换话题时，要有衔接词，不要给人突兀跳转的感觉。写展示大纲是避免以上问题的最好方式。如果你的听众对你的观点抱着愿意接受的态度，你应该选用直接提出观点的方式；如果你的听众抱着怀疑，不接受的态度，则应该将自己的关键主张放在最后。

Example

- Challenges your prospect companies are facing
- Why the typical ways of solving these challenges fail
- Implications and costs of not solving the challenges
- The right way to overcome the challenges
- Very quick overview of how your company helps customers solve these challenges

Why your company? Reason 1; Reason 2; Reason 3

Reason 1

- Why Reason 1 is important
- Process—how you do things to deliver Reason 1
- Statistics—showing how you compare for Reason 1
- Awards or Analyst comments for Reason 1
- Case studies or quotes about how you deliver Reason 1

Reason 2

- Why Reason 2 is important
- Process—how you do things to deliver Reason 2
- Statistics—showing how you compare for Reason 2
- Awards or Analyst comments for Reason 2
- Case studies or quotes about how you deliver Reason 2

Reason 3

- Why Reason 3 is important
- Process—how you do things to deliver Reason 3
- Statistics—showing how you compare for Reason 3
- Awards or Analyst comments for Reason 3
- Case studies or quotes about how you deliver Reason 3

Why your company? Reason 1; Reason 2; Reason 3—Recap

Case writing

Task: Imagine you are the sales manager of a company that sells software for office use. You are going to do a product presentation to your prospective client.

Please outline your presentation in no more than **150** words.

Part F
Further business story

Going Global: The Importance of Cross-Cultural Communication in Business

Today's business landscape is increasingly global. Employees interact with colleagues, customers and prospects from different parts of the world on a daily basis. To successfully compete, business leaders need to have an understanding of the cultural *nuances* of the different regions in which their business operates. Otherwise, they can face misunderstandings, conflict in the workplace and ultimately lost revenue or profit. Plus, lack of understanding of these cultural nuances can create *frustrations* among teams and lead to lower productivity and higher costs. In dealing with customers, a failure to connect may even result in lost opportunities and revenue. As organizations expand globally, partner with foreign companies or complete *mergers* and *acquisitions*, cultural differences are brought to the *forefront*.

Cross-cultural communication is no longer a new idea neither from academic, nor from business *perspective*. Many researchers are interested in this topic, especially that it undergoes a transformation. The way we leave, the way we speak, the way we learn is affecting the way we are doing business.

One of the most important and prominent research was done by Geert Hofstede. IBM asked him to conduct research in all countries they are working in to get to know specifics of particular cultures and groups. Hofstede found out that there are some important dimensions that are influencing our private life as much as work.

The first example might be the power distance dimension. If you are from US or Western Europe probably everyone in your company speak to each other in an informal way using the name or "you" form. The more to the East you go the more hierarchy you see so even in Poland many of your colleagues use the informal way of communication, but the higher in hierarchy you go we use more official form sometimes even with surname. You can find in the Easter Europe examples of firms where people use form like

"Mr. President", "chief" or "boss". Working in the Middle East, Africa and Far East you have to be even more conscious about the forms you are using.

Every region and each country have its specific *honorific* forms we should keep in mind not to make *faux pas* which may cost us a lot, like losing contract. That particular dimension is obviously affecting the way companies and board members are taking decisions.

Another researcher also developing dimensions theory was Edward T. Hall who took notice of the way we perceive the time. Some nations and *monochromic*—cannot leave without calendar and clock—while other are *polychromic*—rather focusing on relations and multi-tasking.

Then, how can we improve cross cultural interactions? There are six secrets to navigating this problem.

1. Take the time to study a colleague's or prospect's culture before a meeting.

Assume that there will likely be some level of disconnect and ask questions during the meeting to clear up any uncertainties. For example, in India, employees are comfortable with some degree of "fuzziness" when it comes to scope of work. However, Americans tend to prefer much more black and white definitions.

2. Be sensitive to differences in the English language.

If you don't, you can easily be *blindsided* by different meanings of words or expressions. For example, when you are working with colleagues in India, pay particular attention to grammatical construction with articles like "the" and "an," among other words as these can pose difficulties for those who speak English as a second language. An Indian speaker may mean to say, "there were a few problems," but actually say, "there were few problems." Without just one little word—a, the meaning of the entire phrase becomes the exact opposite. Understandably, this can lead to a significant misunderstanding if taken out of context.

Even among native English speakers, there are variations in the meaning of certain words. In the US we know that "table it" means let's put it aside. But in the UK, the same phrase means the exact opposite—let's put it on the table and discuss it now.

3. Pay attention to differences in body language across cultures.

During an in-person meeting or phone call, an Indian employee will often nod their head "yes" or make sounds in the affirmative. However, this doesn't actually mean they necessarily agree with you. Rather, this is a gesture to show that they've heard what you said. A Western colleague could easily misconstrue this as agreement and a misunderstanding could ensue.

4. Be aware of various dinner rituals.

Many cross-cultural differences are brought to the forefront at business dinners. In

Eastern cultures, family style dining is the norm. In this context it's not only polite, but a friendly gesture, to share food off your plate—even in a business meeting—which may be a surprise to many Westerners.

Dining in the US can be a challenge for people from Eastern cultures as well. And differences in food and *etiquette* can be made more difficult by a hesitation among many Eastern employees to ask questions, for fear of looking unprepared or unprofessional.

For example, someone from Japan may have never used a lobster cracker before, but they may not want to ask how to. When I'm training employees, I always offer the reminder that there's nothing wrong with asking and that questions will usually be met with enthusiasm from the host in showing you how things are done in their country.

5. Realize business card exchanges are not the same around the world.

Japanese employees will generally bow and provide their card with both hands. It's expected that you accept the card with both hands and then take a few moments to read the card to show respect. In the UK, more than in the US, colleagues will often just place their card on the table in a meeting, with less ceremony involved.

6. Get your company onboard with a cross-cultural awareness program.

By doing so, you can teach your team across regions how to interact effectively. This is especially important when employees are moving overseas, and trainings should include sessions on greetings, business etiquette and dining customs. These training sessions usually lead to many "aha!" moments.

By identifying and embracing these cultural differences rather than ignoring them, organizations can create stronger global teams and better relationships with customers and prospects, allowing them to *thrive* in the global competitive landscape.

New words and expressions

acquisition	n.	获得
blindside	vt.	攻其不备
etiquette	n.	礼节
forefront	n.	最前沿
frustration	n.	挫折
honorific	adj.	尊敬的
merger	n.	合并
monochromic	adj.	单色的
nuance	n.	细微区别
perspective	n.	观点；远景
polychromic	adj.	彩饰的

| thrive | *vi.* | 繁荣，兴旺 |
| faux pas | | 失礼，失态 |

Critical thinking

Work in groups and discuss the following questions.

(1) What are the basic features and major role of economic globalization?

(2) How to solve the problems on cross-cultural barrier?

(3) What information should be included in a sales contract?